American English

BY Albert H. Marckwardt

OXFORD UNIVERSITY PRESS

LONDON   OXFORD   NEW YORK

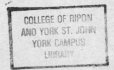

☆ The map which appears on p. 136 is taken from Hans Kurath's *Word Geography of the Eastern United States* and is reproduced by permission of the University of Michigan Press.

This reprint, 1978

FJBN
on b cle
cover

MMR

TO JUDY

PREFACE

ANYONE who has the temerity to come forward with a treatment of American English at this particular time necessarily incurs both a responsibility and a debt. The responsibility is that of saying something that has not been said before. The debt, obviously, is to all of the painstaking and careful scholarship of those who have previously worked in the field.

Whatever claim to originality the present work may have should be sufficiently clear in the pages which follow so as not to require a restatement here. The only point which might be profitably called to the attention of the reader is that the principal aim has been to present a synthesis of the growth and development of the English language in America. If American linguistic scholarship has had one fault in the past, it has been primarily that of collecting isolated facts by the scores and hundreds, and often neglecting to put them together in a consistent and ordered whole. In the main the present study has been content to employ the excellent collections of factual data turned up by the many excellent scholars who have concerned themselves with this subject. It has, however, attempted to see and to present these in the light of a consistent interpretation centering about the fundamental relationship between language and culture.

There is an equal obligation to set forth here the limitations of this study. Though the work is broad in scope, it makes no claim to completeness. To deal in full detail with all the minutiae which are a part of the full story of American English would require more than even the three volumes which Mencken devoted to the subject. The instances of one type of language development or another which appear throughout the book are by no means intended to be exhaustive; they have been selected, instead, as being typical of a much larger number of similar changes or developments. In addition, whole topics—such as immigrant English, slang, and technical vocabularies—have either been omitted entirely or touched upon very slightly because they seem to have only a minor bearing upon the principal thesis: the close interaction of linguistic and cultural factors in the growth of American English. This does not mean that they are unimportant or without interest in their own right.

Nor does the author consider his task here to be that of a propagandist for any type of educational doctrine with reference to school programs in, or school attitudes toward English usage. In fact, the so-called language arts programs in our schools and the attitudes of various sectors of our society toward the English language are a product of our cultural history and development. As such, they are recorded here objectively rather than discussed polemically.

We must also recognize that no native speaker of British English has ever dealt with the American variety of the language to the complete satisfaction of those who speak it as their mother tongue. Conversely, no one born and reared in the United States is likely to satisfy the native Briton with what he has to say about the language as spoken and written in England. This latter could be the understatement of the decade. Yet, if an author is forced to deal in some measure with both varieties of the language, all he can do is to employ every possible caution in treating the one which is not native to him: to consult native speakers whenever possible, to employ the most reliable sources of information, and to document them. These precautions have been taken, but I have no illusions that every reader will agree with all that has been said about either British or American English.

I hasten to say that the present work is indebted to virtually every previous treatment of the subject. Chief among these, of course, are Mencken's *The American Language* and Krapp's *The English Language in America*. Excellent studies of special topics, ranging all the way from that of George R. Stewart on place names to Mamie Meredith's on the nomenclature of fences, are so numerous as to defy mention. Without the mass of thoroughly sifted and carefully presented lexicographical evidence contained in the *Oxford English Dictionary*, the *Dictionary of American English*, and the *Dictionary of Americanisms*, this book could not have been written. Nor should one overlook the splendid service rendered by the journal *American Speech*, in encouraging research and in providing a publication outlet and a forum for discussion. I must not forget to pay a particular tribute to my linguistic colleagues at the University of Michigan, particularly Charles C. Fries and Hans Kurath, not only for their truly outstanding contributions to the study of our language but also for the stimulating and scholarly atmosphere which their presence assures. The assistance I have received from my wife, Grace McCarroll Marckwardt, has been so extensive and varied that it is futile even to attempt to describe it.

Ann Arbor   A.H.M.
January 1958

CONTENTS

AMERICAN ENGLISH

1

The English Language in America

How many people in the world speak English as a first or native language? Exact information on this point is not available, but an estimate of 230 million cannot be very wide of the mark. Of these, 145 million live in the United States, a little less than fifty-five million in the United Kingdom and Ireland, and something like thirty million in the British dominions and colonial possessions. It is even more difficult to arrive at a figure representing those who speak English as a second or auxiliary language. Here the guesses range from fifty million to 125 million. A reasonably conservative conclusion would thus place the total number of speakers of English between 300 million and 325 million, about one-seventh of the world's population.

If one thinks solely in terms of total numbers of speakers, it must be conceded that some authorities place Chinese, the various Indic languages, and Russian ahead of English; others only Chinese. Both Chinese and Indic, however, are terms covering a large number of mutually unintelligible dialects, and though the numbers of speakers of these languages may seem impressive, communication within the languages is much more restricted than in English. Total numbers, moreover, constitute but one phase of the matter. The factor of geographical distribution is equally, possibly even more, significant. English is spoken as a first or native language on at least four continents of the world;

1

Russian on two, Chinese and the Indic languages on one. English is without question the closest approach to a world language today.

It goes without saying that no two persons ever have an identical command of their common language. Certainly they have not precisely the same vocabulary. There are at least minor differences in pronunciation; indeed the same individual will not pronounce his vowels and consonants in absolutely identical fashion every time he utters them. Everyone possesses in addition certain individual traits of grammatical form and syntactical order, constituting that peculiar and personal quality of language which we term style. All of this is implicit in the well-known phrase, "Style is the man." No two men are identical; no two styles are the same. If this be true of but two persons, the potential of difference resident in a language spoken by more than 200 million truly staggers the imagination.

The peculiar use of language characteristic of any one person depends in large part upon such factors as home environment, education, occupation, recreational habits, and the political and social institutions in which he plays a part. Moreover, it is reasonable to assume that speakers with a similar environmental background will be more alike in their language, as in other modes of behavior, than those hailing from widely disparate surroundings. Of the 230 million speakers of English, one group of 145 million possesses many of these environmental factors as a common background. These are the speakers of English who live in the United States. Another group of some fifty million also shares a common environment. They are, of course, the speakers of British English. Upon a priori grounds alone, one would be justified in expecting to find certain characteristic differences between British and American English.

But we need not content ourselves with a priori assumption. Few native Americans who have not lived in England for any great period of time would be able to explain the meaning of *spanner*, of *gearbox*, of a *leat*, a *lasher*, a *switchback*. And even if they can understand such terms as *petrol*, *oddments*, *valuer*,

bus caravan, or *superannuation scheme,* they do not normally
employ them. Nor is this casual collection of Briticisms the result
of any extensive search. Words such as these may be found in
any daily newspaper published in England; they are a part of
the ordinary vocabulary of every speaker of British English. Conversely, then, we in the United States must also be prepared to
recognize that our *monkey wrench, transmission, gasoline, house
trailer,* and *pension plan* will sound quite as strange and unusual
to the average speaker of British English.

There are, of course, constant reminders that these two great
divisions of the English-speaking people do not always understand each other without special effort. American forces stationed
in England during the war were provided with little booklets
indicating some of the outstanding differences between British
and American customs and language. Such novels and plays as
Main Street and *Brother Rat* were supplied with glossaries for
the British trade. In current English novels, statements such as
these often reflect the author's conception of the differences between the two varieties of the English language:*

> 'I'm sorry,' she said in her turn; and relapsing into a rare Amer-
> icanism, 'but that's all there is to it.'

> Camilla refused a taxi, saying, 'The shop's only just around the
> corner.' He chaffed her for the Americanism.

Some years ago Lion Feuchtwanger's novel *The Oppermans*
was translated from the German, first by an Englishman and
then by an American. A comparison of the two versions made
by Professor Edmund E. Miller brings out some interesting differences between American and British vocabulary. The following are some of the variant translations of the same German
word or expression:

* Both passages are from *The Royal Regiment* by Gilbert Frankau.
Whether the supposed Americanisms are really confined to usage in the
United States is beside the point. Both American and English authors are
often notoriously inaccurate in what they conceive to be distinctive British
and American usage respectively.

AMERICAN	ENGLISH
subway train	underground train
furniture store	furnishing stores
newspaper clipping	newspaper cutting
That's tough!	Oh crumbs!
lousy slob	great impudent oaf
from the ground up	down to its last detail
elevator	lift
elevator-boy	lift-boy
It wasn't a picnic.	It wasn't a beanfest.
phonograph records	gramophone records
to have the jitters	to get icebergs down your back
It was nearly six o'clock.	It was getting on for six o'clock.
What did he have to do today?	What had he got to do today?

In this same connection, it is difficult to refrain from mentioning the sign which is supposed to have appeared in a Paris shop window with the legend: ENGLISH SPOKEN—AMERICAN UNDERSTOOD.

It is apparent then that American English does possess certain qualities peculiar to itself. The degree of autochthony which may be ascribed to it has been a matter of some difference of opinion and is strikingly reflected in the titles of the two principal books which have been written on the subject. Shortly after the close of the First World War, H. L. Mencken, who, as co-editor of the magazine *Smart Set*, was then the literary bad boy of the United States, assumed the role of philologist and surprised the world of letters with his book *The American Language*. Six years later, Professor George Philip Krapp of Columbia University published a two-volume work on the same subject, which he called *The English Language in America*.

It is by no means overstraining a point to maintain that the difference in these two titles reflects a thoroughgoing difference in attitude toward the material under consideration. Mencken at that time, with his attention fixed particularly on the spoken language, felt that 'the American form of the English language was plainly departing from the parent stem, and it seemed at least likely that the differences between American and English would go on increasing.' 'This,' he says, 'was what I argued in my first three editions.' Krapp, more concerned with the written, in fact the formal literary language, took the opposite point of view, insisting that 'historical and comparative study brings American English in closer relation to the central tradition of the English language than is commonly supposed to exist.'

American English, the title of the present work, a term also used previously by Gilbert M. Tucker and more recently by Professor Thomas Pyles, reflects a position midway between the two extremes. To apply, as Mencken did, the term *language* to the American variety of English implies a much greater degree of mutual unintelligibility between it and British English than there actually is. A Yorkshireman and an Alabaman will not understand one another easily and without some effort, but they will understand one another. On the other hand, Krapp's title, though satisfactory as a label for his thesis, scarcely suggests enough. English in this country has maintained the 'central tradition' of the English language, but at the same time it has reflected with great fidelity those facets of cultural history and development which are peculiar to our people and our milieu. *American English* suggests precisely this. The term *English* denies the implication of a separate language. At the same time the adjective *American,* unblushingly appropriated, as is our wont, without regard for the feelings of the inhabitants of this continent outside the national borders of the United States, is intended to indicate more than the mere transplanting of a vernacular to a new soil, but rather to suggest its new growth as a somewhat changed and wholly indigenous organism.

This brings us to a statement of the purpose and the point of departure of the present work. Certain characteristic vocabulary differences between British and American English have already been mentioned. That there are also differences in pronunciation is so obvious as to require no demonstration. Close scrutiny will also reveal some minor differences in inflectional pattern and other aspects of grammatical structure. To some extent, therefore, the immense potential of variation in a language with more than 200 million speakers is being realized.

The relationship between language, its vocabulary and structure, and the background and environment of the individual speaker has already been suggested. We may approach this same relationship in a somewhat broader fashion by saying that language is a social tool or a social organism. As such it is the product of the society which employs it, and as it is employed it is engaged in a continual process of re-creation. If this is the case, we may reasonably expect a language to reflect the culture, the folkways, the characteristic psychology of the people who use it.

Given an American English which differs perceptibly from its British counterpart, we come to the question, 'How does this American variety of English reflect those facets of cultural history, institutional development, and physical environment which are peculiar to the English-speaking people on the American continent and which they do not share with speakers of English elsewhere on the globe?' In short, how does American English reflect the American tradition and the American character? And further, what language processes have operated to produce such differences between British and American English, and how have they operated? It is with these particular questions that the various chapters of this book will be concerned.

There is still another aspect of this problem which we can scarcely afford to overlook. American culture is by no means homogeneous; the *Kulturbild* differs in various parts of our country. It is fairly accurate to say that in the United States there are at least six regional cultures: a New England, an Old South, a Middle West, a Rocky Mountain and Great Plains, a Southwest, and a Far West culture. In fact, even these are capable of subdivision.

Moreover, the American English of these regions is not entirely uniform. Everyone is aware that certain features of speech are peculiar to New England and that others are characteristic of the coastal South. Indeed, the language employed in other sections of the country is by no means as lacking in variant features as is sometimes thought. In the light of the approach which has already been outlined with respect to British and American English, it is equally pertinent to ask as well: do the regional differences within American English itself also reflect the differences among these regional cultures?

The question now having been raised in two different ways, externally and internally, so to speak, it remains for us to see what kind of answer can be found. But first we must look a little into the state of the English language at the time when the English-speaking colonies were first established in the New World.

2

The Language of the Colonists

In considering the history and development of American English we must remember that the courageous bands who ventured westward into the unknown with Captain John Smith or on board the *Mayflower,* as well as those who followed them later in the seventeenth century, were speaking and writing the English language as it was currently employed in England. Consequently, whatever linguistic processes operated to produce the differences between American and British English which exist today must either have taken place in American English after the colonists settled on this continent or have occurred in British English after the emigrants left their homeland. Or, as a third possibility, there may have been changes in both divisions of the language after the period of settlement. We cannot, however, escape the conclusion of original identity and subsequent change.

Our first concern, therefore, is with the kind of English spoken by Smith's Virginians, Calvert's Marylanders, the Plymouth Fathers, the Bostonians of the Massachusetts Bay Colony, Roger Williams' Rhode Islanders, and Penn's Quakers. What was the state of the language at the time they left the shores of their native England?

The answer to this entails making a comparison between the

SETTLEMENT OF AMERICA	ENGLISH AUTHORS	ENGLISH WORKS

1600

SHAKESPEARE · BACON · DONNE · JONSON · BROWNE · DEKKER

1607 Jamestown, Virginia

Volpone 1606
Macbeth
Authorized 1611
Version, Bible

MILTON

1620 Plymouth, Mass.
1623 Dover & Portsmouth, N.H.
1624 New Amsterdam, by Dutch

Anatomy of Melancholy 1621
First Folio Shakespeare 1623

BUNYAN

1630 Boston, Mass.
1632 St. Mary's, Maryland
1635 Hartford, Conn.
1636 Providence, R.I.
1638 Delaware, by Swedes
1641 York, Maine

PEPYS · DRYDEN

L'Allegro, Il Penseroso 1634
Religio Medici 1635
Lycidas 1637

Areopagitica 1644

Compleat Angler 1653

1655 Dutch defeat Swedes
in New Jersey

1664 English capture
New Amsterdam

SWIFT · ADDISON · CONGREVE

Essay Dramatic Poesy 1664

Paradise Lost 1667
(published)

1670 Charleston, S.C.

1675 King Philip's War

1681 Pennsylvania, by Quakers

Pilgrim's Progress 1678

Newton, Principia 1687

POPE

Battle of the Books 1697
Way of the World

1700

IMPORTANT DATES IN
THE SETTLEMENT OF AMERICA AND ENGLISH LITERARY HISTORY

memorable dates of our early colonial history with those pertinent to the English literary scene throughout the seventeenth
century. In this connection the tabulation on the preceding page
will prove helpful It shows, for example, that Jonson was at the
height of his career and that Shakespeare was still writing when
Jamestown was settled. Plymouth Colony was founded before
the publication of Shakespeare's First Folio and less than a
decade after the completion of the Authorized Version of the
Bible.

Dryden, who is often called the father of modern prose, was
not born until after the settlement of the second colony in New
England. His *Essay of Dramatic Poesy* was not written until the
capture of New York by the English, nor were the essays of
Cowley, equally modern in style and temper. The publication
date of *Paradise Lost* is somewhat later, and that of *Pilgrim's
Progress* actually follows King Philip's War in point of time. I
mention these in particular because we often think of these last
two works as indicative of the same kind of dissent against the
Anglican Church as that which is reflected in the colonial settlement, particularly in the north. Yet Massachusetts, Connecticut,
and Rhode Island were all established and flourishing by the
time these books appeared. Even such late prose representative
of Elizabethan exuberance, complication, involution, and to some
extent lack of discipline as Burton's *Anatomy of Melancholy* and
Browne's *Religio Medici* postdate the establishment of the early
New England settlements.

The émigrés who accompanied Smith and Bradford had
learned their native language long before the years 1607 and
1620 respectively. Many of them were mature; some were old.
Even a man of forty on the Jamestown expedition would presumably have learned to speak English about 1570; John Rolfe, the
future husband of Pocahontas, acquired his native tongue probably in 1587. A young man of twenty-one, John Alden for example, in the Mayflower company must have learned English at the
height of Shakespeare's career; Miles Standish, when Shakespeare was beginning to write. In short, the earliest English colo-

nists in the New World were speaking Elizabethan English, the language of Shakespeare, Lyly, Marlowe, Lodge, and Green, when they came to America—not the measurably different English of Dryden, Defoe, and Bunyan. This is important and necessary for our understanding of some of the distinctive features which American English was to develop later on.

Next, what was the general state of Elizabethan English? How many people spoke it? The population of England, excluding Ireland and Scotland, in Shakespeare's time has been estimated at 4,460,000. This is a little more than the present population of Massachusetts, somewhat less than that of Michigan. Of these, probably 200,000 lived in London in 1600; the population in 1605 is given as 224,275. This is approximately the population of Syracuse, New York, or of Oklahoma City. These people and possibly 25,000 more in the immediate vicinity spoke London English, the regional variety which was in the process of becoming a standard for the English-speaking world as a whole.

Naturally the language sounded somewhat different from its twentieth-century counterpart. Certain though not all of these differences provide us with a partial explanation of the current variations in pronunciation between British and American English. For one thing, many words which are now pronounced with the vowel of *meat* had, at the time of the earliest settlements in America, the quality of present-day English *mate*. In fact, Londoners were accustomed to hear both the *ee* and the *ay* sounds in such words as *meat, teach, sea, tea, lean,* and *beard.* The conservative *ay* pronunciation continued in the language as late as the time of Pope. On occasion Shakespeare was capable of rhyming *please* with *knees* and at other times with *grace.* Without this double pronunciation a speech such as that by Dromio, 'Marry sir, she's the Kitchin wench, & al *grease* (*grace*)' would have lost its punning effect.

It is quite possible that words which today have the vowel of *mate* were also pronounced at times with the vowel of *sand.* In addition to the play on the words *grease* and *grace* cited in the foregoing paragraph, there is in *All's Well* another punning

passage involving a common or highly similar pronunciation of
grace and *grass*:

> CLOWN.   Indeed sir she was the sweete margerom of the sallet
> or rather the hearbe of grace.
> LAFEW.   They are not hearbes you knave, they are nose-
> hearbes.
> CLOWN.   I am no great Nebuchadnezar sir, I have not much
> skill in grace.

A rhyme such as the following from *Venus and Adonis* suggests the same conclusion:

> Even so poor birds, deceived with painted grapes . . .
> Even so she languisheth in her mishaps.

There was undoubtedly quite as much fluctuation in words
which are generally spelled with *oo*; those of the *food, good,* and
flood classes respectively. It is only recently that the pronunciation of many of these words has become standardized. All three
of these words constitute one of Shakespeare's rhymes, and a
half-century later Dryden rhymed *flood* with *mood* and *good.*
Even today certain words of this class (*roof, room, root, hoof,
coop, soot,* etc.) are pronounced variously in different parts of
the United States.

At the time of which we are writing, the vowel of *cut* had but
recently developed in London speech and was not yet a feature
of all the English dialects. Combinations of *ir, er,* and *ur* in words
like *bird, learn,* and *turn* had not long before coalesced into a
vowel which was more like the sound to be heard over most
of the United States today than that which is characteristic of
southern British English. Contemporary pronunciation was far
from settled in words like *clerk,* which seemed to be classed part
of the time with the sound of *dark* and at other times with the
vowel of *jerk.* Moreover, this variation affected many more words
than it does now. Shakespeare rhymed *convert* with *art, serve*
with *carve, heard* with *regard.*

In addition, the language at that time had no sound like the stressed vowel of present-day *father* or *calm*. The diphthongs characteristic of such words as *house* and *loud* had, instead of the *ah* first element commonly employed today, a sound something like the final vowel of *Cuba*. The whole diphthong was pronounced in a manner quite similar to that which may be heard at the present time in tidewater Virginia or in the Toronto area. The diphthong in words like *bite* and *bide* began with this same neutral element. The so-called short *o* sound of *cot* and *fog* was always pronounced with the lips somewhat rounded, as in Modern English *fall.**

Nor were the stress patterns of Shakespeare's English absolutely identical with those of the modern period. A line such as 'The light will show, character'd in my brow,' indicates clearly that in such a trisyllabic word as *character'd,* the stress had not yet shifted to the first syllable. A good many two-syllable words which now stress the first, at that time had the accent on the second. Note, 'And there I'll rest, as after much *turmoil.*' Many derivatives in *-able* had a distinct stress, at least secondary in value, on the suffix. A line such as 'What *acceptable* audit canst thou leave?' can scarcely be read in any other fashion.

Many words show a double stress pattern: *sincere* with stress at times on the first and at times on the second syllable; *confiscate* on occasion has initial stress, and elsewhere on the second syllable. It is probably fair to say that just as with vowel quality, the language during the Elizabethan period permitted somewhat more latitude than it does today.

It must be kept in mind, moreover, that the pronunciations which have just been discussed reflect only the language practices of the inhabitants of London and its environs, constituting approximately 5 per cent of the five million who spoke English at that time. The remaining 95 per cent spoke the regional or

---

* For those who would like a more comprehensive treatment of Elizabethan pronunciation, a phonetic transcription of one of the well-known passages from Shakespeare's *As You Like It* has been supplied in the appendix.

provincial dialects. Those who live in the United States find it hard to conceive of the extent to which regional dialects may differ even today within an area no larger than one of our moderate-size states.

At the present time, to select just a single instance, a word such as *about* will be pronounced with the stressed vowel of *bite* in Devon, with the vowel of *boot* along the Scottish border, with the vowel of *father* and a final consonant more like *d* than *t* in London Cockney, and with a pronunciation something like *abaeut* in Norfolk.

To anyone who has grown up in a tradition of relative linguistic uniformity over a territory virtually three million square miles in area, such differences in speech present in a country only one-sixtieth as large are startling, to say the least. But in the England of today, regional dialects are confined to a relatively small portion of the population as compared with three centuries ago. There can be little question about the wide prevalence of dialect and the general lack of uniformity of speech among the vast majority of the settlers of the seventeenth century.

Seventeenth-century English differed from its modern counterpart in other aspects of speech as well. Although the language had in general developed most of the inflections which are used in present-day English—the noun plurals, the object form *them* in the plural pronoun, the past tense and past participle forms of the weak verb—a few interesting earlier features still remained. Among these were the double forms of the pronoun of address: *thou* and *ye* or *you*. Because the distribution of these was governed partly by considerations of social rank and in part on the basis of emotional overtones, their very presence in the language made for a subtlety which today must be achieved through quite different means. Note, for example, in the following well-known passage from the first part of *Henry IV*, how the choice of pronouns reflects Hotspur's shift of mood from jesting concealment to stern warning, concluding with a gentler and more intimate tone:

> Come, wilt *thou* see me ride?
> And when I am o'horseback, I will swear
> I love *thee* infinitely. But hark *you*, Kate;
> I must not have *you* henceforth question me
> Whither I go, nor reason whereabout.
> Whither I must, I must; and, to conclude,
> This evening must I leave *you*, gentle Kate.
> I know *you* wise; but yet no farther wise
> Than Harry Percy's wife. Constant *you* are,
> But yet a woman; and for secrecy,
> No lady closer; for I well believe
> *Thou* wilt not utter what *thou* dost not know;
> And so far will I trust *thee*, gentle Kate.

And again in Kate's preceding speech but one, her change from exasperation to gentle entreaty is indicated in precisely the same manner.

> Come, come, *you* paraquito, answer me
> Directly unto this question that I ask.
> In faith, I'll break *thy* little finger, Harry,
> An if *thou* wilt not tell me all things true.

Actually, at one point slightly later than Shakespeare's time, this matter of the second personal pronoun became a politico-religious issue. The Quakers, committed to a belief in the innate equality of all men, interpreted the duality of the pronoun of address as a negation of that equality and argued, quite intemperately at times, for a return to an older state of the language where the two forms were differentiated solely on the basis of number. In the following passage, George Fox, the founder and leader of the sect, set forth his views in no uncertain terms.

Do not they speak false English, false Latine, false Greek . . . and false to the other Tongues, . . . that doth not speak *thou* to *one*, what ever he be, Father, Mother, King, or Judge; is he not a Novice and Unmannerly, and an Ideot and a Fool, that speaks *You* to *one*, which is not to be spoken to a *singular*, but to many? O Vulgar Professors and Teachers, that speaks

Plural when they should Singular . . . Come you Priests and
Professors, have you not learnt your Accidence?

It is worth noting that the English language did eventually go
along with Fox's democratic notions by giving up the pronoun
differentiation based upon social status, but in so doing, ironically selected the form which he considered inappropriate for
the task.

This double supply of pronouns also carried with it an accompanying difference in verb structure, for *thou* as subject regularly demanded a verb ending in -*est*. *Ye* or *you* as subjects were
accompanied merely by the simple or root form of the verb.
Thus we would have had at this time *thou teachest* but *ye* or *you*
teach, thou knowest but *you know*. After the *thou* forms fell into
disfavor, so too did the verb inflections in -*est*, leaving the second
person singular of the verb identical with the first person and
with all forms of the plural.

In addition Elizabethan English represents a period of change
from an earlier -*eth* inflection for the third person singular of the
verb to the -*s* forms characteristic of the language today. There
is an interesting difference here between the practice of Shakespeare and that of the contemporary King James Version of the
Bible. The latter regularly uses -*eth*: 'He maketh me to lie down
in green pastures.' In his ordinary dramatic prose, Shakespeare
employs -*s* regularly for all verbs except *have* and *do*, which
retain the archaic *hath* and *doth* (the latter only occasionally)
presumably because these were learned as individual forms early
in life by the average speaker instead as part of an over-all
pattern.

Even here, however, one must exercise due caution in inter-
preting the -*eth* spellings. In the middle of the seventeenth
century one Richard Hodges wrote *A Special Help to Orthogra-
phie*, which consisted chiefly in listing words 'alike in sound but
unlike both in their signification and writing.' Among the
homophonic pairs which appear in this treatise are *roweth* and

rose, wrights and *righteth,* Mr. *Knox* and *knocketh.* He goes on
to say in explanation:

> Therefore, whensoever *eth* cometh in the end of any word,
> wee may pronounce it sometimes as *s,* and sometimes like *z,*
> as in these words, namely, in *bolteth it,* and *boldeth it,* which
> are commonly pronounc't, as if they were written thus, *bolts*
> it, and *bolds* it: save onely in such words, where either *c, s,*
> *sh, ch, g,* or *x* went before it: as in *graceth, pleaseth, washeth,*
> *matcheth, rageth, taxeth*: for, these must still remaine as two
> syllables. Howbeit, if men did take notice, how they use to
> speak, in their ordinary speech to one another, they might
> plainly perceive, that in stead of *graceth,* they say *graces,* and
> so they pronounce al other words of this kinde, accordingly.

Unquestionably the best way to acquire a feeling for many
of the differences between the language of today and that of
the age of Elizabeth is to observe with some care a selection of
one of the earliest examples of what might be called American
English. The following selection from William Bradford's *History
of Plimmoth Plantation* will serve the purpose:

> In these hard and difficulte beginnings they found some dis-
> contents and murmurings arise amongst some, and mutinous
> speeches and carriages in other; but they were soone quelled
> and overcome by the wisdome, patience, and just and equall
> carrage of things by the Gov[erno]r and better part, which
> clave faithfully togeather in the maine. But that which was
> most sadd and lamentable was, that in 2 or 3 moneths time
> halfe of their company dyed, espetialy in Jan: and February,
> being the depth of winter, and wanting houses and other com-
> forts; being infected with the scurvie and other diseases, which
> this long voiage and their inacomodate condition had brought
> upon them; so as ther dyed some times 2 or 3 of a day, in the
> aforesaid time; that of 100 and odd persons, scarce 50 re-
> mained. And of these in the time of most distres, ther was but
> 6 or 7 sound persons, who, to their great comendations be it
> spoken, spared no pains, night nor day, but with abundance
> of toil and hazard of their owne health, fetched them woode,
> made them fires, drest them meat, made their beads, washed

their lothsome cloaths, cloathed and uncloathed them; in a
word, did all the homly and necessarye offices for them which
dainty and quesie stomacks cannot endure to hear named; and
all this willingly and cherfully, without any grudging in the
least, shewing herin their true love unto their freinds and
bretheren. A rare example and worthy to be remembered. Tow
of these 7 were Mr. William Brewster, ther reverend Elder,
and Myles Standish, ther Captein and Military comander, unto
whom my selfe, and many others, were much beholden in our
low and sicke condition. And yet the Lord so upheld these
persons, as in this generall calamity they were not at all in-
fected either with sickness, or lamnes. And what I have said
of these, I may say of many others who dyed in this generall
visitation, and others yet living, that whilst they had health,
yea, or any strength continuing, they were not wanting to any
that had need of them. And I doute not but their recompence
is with the Lord.

But I may not hear pass by an other remarkable passage
not to be forgotten. As this calamitie fell among the passengers
that were to be left here to plant, and were hasted a shore and
made to drinke water, that the sea-men might have the more
bear, and one in his sickness desiring but a small cann of beere,
it was answered, that if he were their owne father he should
have none; the disease begane to fall amongst them also, so as
allmost halfe of their company dyed before they went away,
and many of their officers and lustyest men, as the boatson,
gunner, 3 quarter-maisters, the cooke, and others. At which
the m[aste]r was something strucken and sent to the sick a
shore and tould the Gov[erno]r he should send for beer for
them that had need of it, though he drunke water homward
bound.

Most noticeable, perhaps, in the passage just quoted are a
number of words no longer current in the language. Among
them are *inacomodate* and *hasted. Yea, unto,* and *beholden* are
rarely employed except in certain set phrases and at times in
religious connections. Other words have come to be used in
contexts quite unlike those in which they appear in this passage.
For instance, *carriages* no longer signifies behavior in the ab-
stract sense; *clothed,* here meaning the specific act of dressing,
has become more general in its use. *Offices* is used here in the

sense of services; *lustiest* to mean healthiest. Though by no means inclusive, these examples suggest the changes which have taken place in the English vocabulary during the last three centuries, both with respect to the words it comprises and the meanings of these words.

Likewise, certain changes in the forms of words have taken place. Almost at the beginning of the passage, *other* was used as a plural pronoun, although the modern form *others* appears later on. *Scarce*, in an adverbial use, indicates that the fetish of the *-ly* ending was somewhat less strong at that time than it is at present. As might be expected, the most pronounced differences are in the verb forms, where *clave* and *drunke* appear as past tenses and *strucken* as a past participle.

Differences in syntax are even more numerous. The plural form of the abstractions *discontents* and *murmurings* would be unlikely to appear in present-day usage, as would *commendations*. Closely connected with this same problem of number is the lack of agreement between subject and verb in, 'There was but 6 or 7 sound persons.' The word *as* in constructions like, 'so as ther dyed,' and 'as in this generall calamity,' would today be replaced by *that*. At the same time, certain pronominal uses of *that* in this selection would unquestionably call for *who* in the language of today.

Even more striking than any of these features is the sentence structure. In general the sentences lack unity and are replete with dangling phrases and clauses. The first sentence in the selection contains fifty-three words, the second eighty-three, and the third attains a total of one hundred and six. These are all long according to modern standards. Ironically enough, the third sentence is followed by an eight word fragment that does not fit the modern pattern of the conventional sentence at all. In the second sentence the parallelism of the phrases introduced by *being* and *wanting* is faulty. The majority of the sentences are without coherence and direction in the present sense of these terms.

The proper conclusion, however, is not that Bradford was a

bad writer—in fact he was not—but that there were differences between seventeenth-century prose and our own. Some of these differences are purely a matter of historical development. The roots of our modern forms and practices were already in the language. It is even more important to recognize this as a period prior to a certain codification, settlement, one might almost say a jelling, of English written prose. A man's spelling was still his own concern, as is clearly evident, and so too, to some extent, were his sentences. If this codification or jelling took place after the two speech areas, England and America, were already separated, it is more than possible that the settling processes might not work out in the same way in both places.

Consequently, since the earliest American settlers employed Elizabethan English, it is the highly variable and complex character of that medium that provides us with an explanation of the beginning of the divergence in the two great streams of our language. It remains to be seen how, and through what means, this divergence developed throughout the course of the intervening centuries.

3

The Melting Pot

Considered from the point of view of vocabulary, there are few 'pure' languages. English has been notorious as a word borrower, but it is safe to say that every one of the Western European tongues has supplemented its word stock by adoptions from other languages. Loan words occur in the languages of aboriginal peoples. Even Indo-European, the parent of most of the languages found today in Europe and many in western Asia, appears to have borrowed words some 4000 years ago from Finno-Ugric, and to have furnished others in return.

One great impetus toward word borrowing arises from the necessity of talking about new things, qualities, operations, concepts, and ideas. Inevitably the movement of a people to a markedly different environment not only creates a problem of communication but makes it urgent. Almost as soon as he struck land, Columbus 'seized by force several Indians on the first island in order that they might learn from us, and in like manner tell us about those things in these lands of which they themselves had knowledge; and the plan succeeded, for in a short time we understood them and they us, sometimes by gesture and signs, sometimes by words; and it was a great advantage to us.'

The migration of the English to North America, the first stage in what was to culminate in a dramatic sweep across the continent, posed quite the same problems and created the same

21

vocabulary need. As soon as the members of the Smith and Bradford companies put themselves ashore in Virginia and Massachusetts respectively, they encountered plants and animals which were new to them. Some of the fish they caught in the coastal waters were unlike anything they had seen before. The land was occupied by tribes of indigenous peoples who spoke strange languages, wore strange clothing, prepared strange foods, maintained tribal customs different from anything the English had previously encountered. Even the landscape was measurably different from the neatly tailored English countryside. Names had to be provided for all these aspects of their new life.

Nor was this situation confined to the original settlement of the Atlantic seaboard. It was constantly repeated as colonization proceeded westward. The fauna and flora of the prairie states, of the deep South, of the Rocky Mountain area, of the Southwest, and of the Pacific coast presented new naming problems, as did the other features of colonial and frontier life.

To take just a single instance, the Lewis and Clark expedition, ostensibly political and economic in purpose, also had a scientific aim. President Jefferson, a man of wide curiosity, eager to learn as much as he possibly could about the newly acquired Louisiana Purchase, enjoined upon the leaders the task of ascertaining the geography of the country, the nature and way of life of the Indian nations, the plants, animals, mineral resources, and the climate. It was thus quite natural that in the notebooks of the members of the expedition, one would find such statements as, 'These natives have a large quantity of this root bread which they call *commass* [camass],' and that subsequent references to the plant would employ the same word.

I. INDIAN INFLUENCE

But before we take up the specific loan words themselves, a few facts about the American Indians and their languages are pertinent.

Estimates place the Indian population of what is now the
United States at 846,000 at the close of the fifteenth century. It
is not likely that there was any considerable increase during the
next 125 years, although some authorities place the number of
Indians in 1600 at 1,300,000. These million Indians spoke something like 350 languages belonging to some twenty-five families,
which at the least were probably as different as the Germanic
and Slavic, or the Celtic and Romance tongues. This means that
the total number of speakers of many of the languages was relatively small, and also that the English-speaking settlers came
into contact with a large number of different languages.

Among the principal families of Indian languages were the
Algonquian, the Iroquoian, the Muskoghian, the Siouan, the
Uto-Aztecan, and the Penutian. The Algonquian languages included, among others, Narragansett, Massachusetts, and Penob-
scot, spoken in New England, Virginian and Powhatan in the
upper South, and Ojibwa and Pottawatomi in the central West.
Languages belonging to the Iroquoian family were distributed
chiefly throughout New York, Pennsylvania, and Ohio, but
Cherokee, spoken in the South, was also one of them. The Muskoghian languages were spoken principally in the deep South;
among them were Seminole, Creek, and Choctaw. The Siouan
languages were to be found chiefly in the plains area west of
the Mississippi, but Catawba and Saponi, spoken in Virginia
and North Carolina likewise belonged to this family. To the
southwest were the Uto-Aztecan languages, their territory pene-
trating deep into Mexico, and finally the Penutian languages
extended over the great Northwest. Individual languages of
these far-flung families furnished most of the American Indian
words which were taken over into English.

In order to understand certain aspects of the borrowing process
we must know something about the nature of these languages as
well. Many of them contain sounds which do not occur in English: series of nasalized vowels and various kinds of pharyn-
gialized and glottalized consonants. Speakers of English would
tend to approximate such sounds rather than to reproduce them.

Frequent also were combinations of consonants absent from
English, such as the initial clusters in the following Ojibwa
words: *mtik, pshikye, kchimkwa.* The English speaker, encoun-
tering such combinations as these, would in all probability
eliminate one of the consonants, or else insert vowels between
them.

Moreover, most of the Indian languages are of the so-called
incorporating type, tending partially though not absolutely to
the sentence word. At the very least, they put together in a
single word a great many elements which with us are separate
lexical units. Inflectionally, they make use not only of suffixes
and prefixes but of infixes as well. William Penn's description,
technically inexact to be sure, undoubtedly reflects the impression that these languages made upon many of the English who
found it necessary to bridge the communication gap:

> Their *Language* is lofty, yet narrow, but like the *Hebrew;* in
> Signification full; like *Short-hand* in writing; *one* word serveth
> in the place of *three,* and the rest are supplied by the under-
> standing of the Hearer: Imperfect in their *Tenses,* wanting in
> their *Moods, Participles, Adverbs, Conjunctions, Interjections:*
> I have made it my business to understand it, that I might not
> want an interpreter on any occasion: And I must say, that I
> know not a Language spoken in *Europe,* that hath words of
> more sweetness or greatness, in *Accent* and *Emphasis,* than
> theirs.

At all events, it was inevitable that Indian words would be
changed considerably, both in form and meaning, as a result of
the borrowing process.

The following list contains the principal loan words in present-
day American English from the various Indian languages of the
North American continent, classified according to the aspects of
life and fields of activity they represent.

This list of American Indian borrowings comprises about
fifty words. I have attempted to include only those which might
be considered part of the current vocabulary of a large number
of speakers of American English, but with this selective aim

TREES, PLANTS, FRUITS

catalpa
catawba
hickory
pecan
persimmon
poke (-berry, -weed)
scuppernong
sequoia
squash
tamarack

ANIMALS

cayuse
chipmunk
moose
muskrat
opossum
raccoon
skunk
terrapin
woodchuck

FISH

menhaden
muskellunge
porgy *
quahog

POLITICAL TERMS

caucus †
mugwump
Tammany

FOODS

hominy
hooch
pemmican
pone
succotash
supawn

AMERINDIAN CULTURE

manitou
pot latch
powwow
sachem
skookum
totem

papoose
squaw

mackinaw
moccasin
tomahawk
wampum

hogan
igloo
kayak
tepee
wigwam

MISCELLANEOUS

chautauqua
chinook
podunk

* This probably represents a mixed derivation or confusion of Spanish *pargo* and a form *paugie* of Narraganset origin.
† The Amerindian origin of this word has recently been called into question. Since no convincing case has been put forward for any other specific derivation, it is included here.

certain difficulties present themselves. Often plant and animal names are current only in the regions where the objects themselves are to be found. Thus *scuppernong, cayuse,* and *menhaden* are likely to be better known in the coastal South, the West, and New England respectively than in other parts of the country. Certain other words, such as *quahog, supawn,* and *chinook,* are still more localized in their distribution and may have alternate terms even within the relatively restricted area where they are current. *Quahog,* for example, alternates with *round clam, hardshell clam,* and *hen clam; hasty pudding, Indian pudding, Indian meal pudding,* and *mush* are all lexical variants of *supawn* in the Hudson Valley.

In addition, many of the Indian borrowings are now disappearing from the language. It was not so long ago that *kinnikinnick* and *poggamoggan* were as familiar at least as the term *pemmican.* They are decidedly less so now. How rapidly these words are dropping from the language is dramatically illustrated by a listing, made in 1902, of borrowings from the Algonquian languages alone. The list contains 132 words. Today not more than thirty-seven of them are in current use.

The headings, which indicate the spheres of life represented by the borrowings, show that the largest number of loan words are connected with Indian institutions and civilization. Here it was obviously easier to borrow the Indian term than to create a new one out of English elements. For the most part the remaining words are the names of plants, animals, and foods which the colonists found in the new world and which were new to them.

Of the fifty-two words included in the list, approximately three-quarters have been derived from one or another of the Algonquian languages. Among the other families represented are Muskoghian, Iroquois, Sioux, Penutian, and Eskimo, but no one of them by more than three. This overwhelming influence of the Algonquian may be explained in part by the fact that these languages were the first to be encountered by the white men as they settled on the Atlantic coast. Once the Algonquian terms had been applied to the unfamiliar fauna, flora, and Indian institutions, they tended to remain in the language, even though words for these same things from other language families were encountered later on. *Wigwam,* an Algonquian term for an Indian house or tent, appears in English as early as 1628, not long after the beginning of the New England colonization. A somewhat different type of lodge, usually conical in shape and more likely to be constructed of skins, was the *tepee* of the plains Indians. The first citation for this is 1835, at a time when explorers and settlers were pushing across the Mississippi. *Hogan,* the Navaho word for a dwelling built of earth and supported by upright or slanting timbers, does not put in an appearance until 1871. Here the various objects differed from each other to a degree, but *wigwam,* the earliest of the borrowings, was frequently used as a synonym for the others.

It is also noteworthy that word borrowing from the Indians began very early. *Moose, raccoon, opossum, terrapin,* and *persimmon* are all recorded prior to the landing of the Pilgrims. *Powwow, sachem, wigwam,* and *musquash* (the earlier form of *muskrat*) were in the language before the founding of the Massachusetts Bay Colony. On the whole, just about one-half of all the American Indian loan words now current in the language became a part of it during the seventeenth century; the other half may be divided about equally between eighteenth-century and nineteenth-century adoptions. There were many more later borrowings of course—sixty-seven have been found in the journals of the members of the Lewis and Clark expedition alone—but many of these words, such as *wapatoo, carkajou,* and *salal,* were of short duration in the English language.

Some of the structural peculiarities of the American Indian languages and the unusual sounds and combinations of sounds they employed have already been mentioned. Since most languages tend to remake or re-form borrowed words in terms of their own general structure, it was natural that these words should have been changed considerably in the borrowing process, usually in the direction of simplification and shortening. According to Roger Williams, the Narragansett word which gave rise to present English *menhaden* was *munnawhatteaug. Wampum* is an abbreviated form of *wampampeag. Squash* appears to have been shortened from a Narragansett *askutasquash. Raccoon* shows up as *raughroughcums* in Captain John Smith's *True Relation*, presumably derived from a Virginian *arahkunem.* Thus it is apparent that either or both ends of a word might be lopped off in the course of the borrowing process. Just how much the actual sounds themselves were altered, we shall probably never know, since the earliest records of the American Indian languages antedate the development of modern phonetic science.

One other type of change may occur in the form of a loan word, the result of a psychological rather than a phonetic process. This is particularly well illustrated by the term *woodchuck,* which seems to have had its origin in a Cree or Ojibwa word appearing variously as *wuchak, otchak, odjig,* meaning 'fisher' or 'weasel.' It was, at any rate, an animal which bore some association with the woods, and presumably to give a semblance of reason to this strange combination of sounds, the English-speaking colonists converted the first syllable into *wood.* This type of modification, arising from a popular or unlearned effort to resolve a strange or unusual word into understandable elements, is called folk or popular etymology.*

Among other possible instances of folk etymology among the Amerindian loan words is *muskrat,* a rodent with a musky odor, called *muskwessu* or *muscassus,* in the Algonquian languages. *Musquash,* the direct reflex of the etymological form, is still regularly employed in England, but the American *muskrat* certainly suggests a reworking of the word in an effort to lend some sense to the component elements. *Chipmunk,* from an Ojibwa *achitam,* may represent the same process. Among Indian words no longer current, Narragansett *wattap,* 'string roots of spruce used for sewing canoes,' often appeared as *watape* or *way-tape.*

---

* It was this process which centuries ago gave us *belfry,* though the word originally had nothing to do with bells, *crayfish,* with no etymological relationship to fish, and *salt cellar,* which bore no affinity with the word for basement.

In words borrowed from such familiar languages as Latin, French, and Italian, there is often a reasonably close correspondence between the meaning of the word in English and in the language from which it was borrowed. Thus *nocturnal, consommé,* and *cupola* have the same meaning in English that they have or had in the languages from which they were taken. Because of the totally different structure of the various American Indian languages, such correspondence between the English and the etymological meaning is much less frequently encountered. Thus *squash* is a clipped form of a Narragansett *askútasquash,* meaning literally 'vegetables eaten green.' *Succotash* is taken from a *misikquatash,* also Narragansett, which signified 'the grains are whole.' Virginian *pawcohiccora,* the original of *hickory,* was a term applied to a hickory or walnut kernel mush, and the word which gave rise to present-day *moose* meant 'he strips or eats off.' In considering borrowings from languages with structures not too different from English it is at least possible to argue for some sort of correspondence in meaning between a loan word and its etymon, ridiculous as these arguments sometimes become. But with languages as totally different in structure from English as those of the Amerindians, the grounds for such an insistence vanish altogether, and indeed the argument is never advanced.

Loan words not only alter their meaning in the course of the borrowing process, but they are equally liable to change after they have become a naturalized part of the English language. *Powwow,* one of the very early American Indian adoptions, originally bore its etymological meaning of priest or medicine man. Less than fifty years from the time of its first appearance in English it was applied to a ceremony in which magic was practiced and feasting and dancing indulged in. About a century later it changed its meaning to that of a council held by Indians or a conference with them, presumably because feasting and dancing were an integral part of such conclaves. After another half-century (1812) the word was so generalized that it was variously applied to political or scientific conferences, friendly consultations, or a palaver of any kind. This final development was actually anticipated by the verb *to powwow*, which was formed from the noun very soon after its adoption into the language.

Equally interesting is the semantic development of *mugwump*. It came from *mugquomp*, a Natick word meaning 'great chief,' and Eliot in his *Massachusetts Bible* used it to translate *duke* in Genesis xxxvi.15. By 1832 the word had acquired an aura of playfulness and jocularity, as illustrated by a citation mentioning the 'most Worshipful Mugwumps of the Cabletow.' In 1884 it was specifically applied by the regular Republicans to those bolters from the party who refused to accept Blaine as the presidential candidate, throwing their support to Cleveland, the Democratic nominee. The element of ridicule and irony intended here may well have gone awry, for Cleveland and not Blaine won the election. At any rate it has since been used, often in a thoroughly complimentary fashion, to indicate an independent in politics, though the recent folk-etymological analysis of the term as one who has his mug on one side of the fence and his 'wump' on the other has again given it a jocular and somewhat unfavorable connotation.

Sachem illustrates a similar development. It originally meant the head of a particular confederation, but it soon changed to the generalized meaning of any great man. This in turn has been specialized to apply to the head of the Tammany political organization.

Another broad type of meaning change is afforded by the development of words which were originally tribal or place names. *Mackinaw*, the name of the island at the junction of Lakes Huron and Michigan, according to one explanation at least, was a shortening of *Michilimackinac*, 'great turtle.' The reason for this application is clear enough to anyone who has suddenly come upon the pine-wooded hills of the island projecting from the water. Under both the British and the American administrations it was the seat of an Indian agency. Here the United States government distributed, among other things, blankets to the Indians, who had a decided preference for plaids, checks, and bright colors. Thus, highly colored blankets intended for Indian distribution came to be known as *Mackinaw blankets*. After the northern part of Michigan became a lumbering center, such blankets frequently furnished the material for short jackets worn by the lumbermen. These were first called *Mackinaw coats*, and finally just *mackinaws*.

In much the same fashion *catawba*, meaning 'separated,' was applied in turn to a Siouan tribe living in Carolina, then to a grape grown in that particular area, next to the wine made from the grape, and finally to the red color characteristic of the wine. *Chinook*, also originally a tribal label, has become the name of a language, two different kinds of winds, and a variety of salmon. Other words present equally fascinating change in meaning stories, but these should be sufficient to make the point that once a foreign word is adopted into the language, it is liable to the application of all the forces making for semantic development and alteration.

In considering the subsequent history of any particular group of loan words within a language, it is always pertinent to observe the particular parts of speech represented by these borrowings. Without exception all the Amerindian loan words are nouns, indicating in a sense the most superficial type of borrowing and reflecting a casual rather than an intimate mingling of the two cultures. However, just as native English words do from time to time change their grammatical functions, so may the borrowed terms, once they have become a part of the language. Eight of the Indian borrowings have become verbs, among them *caucus*, *powwow*, *tomahawk*, *hickory*, *skunk* (in a slang sense), *wigwam*, *potlatch*, and *mugwump*, although the last three are certainly rarely used. In general the conversion to verbal use occurred not long after the original noun adoption—within half a century in the case of most of these, and sometimes in considerably less time.

Although functional change of the noun-verb type is relatively infrequent, most of the borrowed nouns entered readily into compound-word combinations. *Webster's New International Dictionary* lists twenty-one compounds for *hickory*, fourteen for *squaw*, sixteen for *skunk*. *Poke* exists only in such combinations as *pokeweed* and *pokeberry*. Sometimes the compounds are triple in nature, as in *hickory leaf borer*, *hickory horned devil*, *hickory gall aphid*.

Certain of these borrowings, although they do not combine extensively with other full words, do show a strong tendency toward the attachment of derivative prefixes and suffixes, particularly the latter. Thus *caucus* has given rise to *caucusable*, *caucusdom*, *caucuser*, *caucusian*, and *caucusified*, to say nothing of *caucusing* as a verbal noun. From *mugwump* we have *mugwumpery*, *mugwumpian*, *mugwumpey*, and *mugwumpism*; from *skunk*, *skunkery*, *skunkish*, and *skunky*. *Tammany* has given us *Tammanyism*, *Tammanyite*, *Tammanyize*, and *Tammanize*. These processes are important for they are a means of greatly increasing the total impact of a group of borrowed words upon the language. By the time all functional changes, compounds, and derivatives are taken into account, something less than fifty loan words have added many times that number of lexical units to the language. According to one estimate, present-day English contains some 1700 words from the Indian languages. This number does seem incredibly large. It is doubtful if any figure can be authoritatively set, but the important point to recognize is that the increase over the actual number of words directly borrowed comes as a result of the processes which have just been discussed.

In addition to the impact upon English produced by the direct borrowings from the Amerindian languages, there were also results of a somewhat more indirect nature. Most obvious of these are the many compounds with the word *Indian* as a first element. Though resulting from a geographical misconception, they would never have been called into existence at all had it not been for the contact with the various American Indian peoples. There are four closely printed columns of these in the *Webster's New International Dictionary*, and although some of them are Indic in their reference, the vast majority—including

Indian claim, Indian summer, Indian file, Indian gift and *giver, Indian creeper,* and *Indian cucumber*—are clearly American in origin. The *Dictionary of American English* lists eighty, the earliest, *Indian field* and *Indian meal,* with citation dates of 1634 and 1635 respectively, testifying to the fact that this process, too, was almost as old as the colonization itself.

Another Amerindian influence may be seen in certain word or phrase combinations which would appear to be the translation into native elements of real or imagined Indian compounds. *Firewater,* for example, is apparently a literal translation of an Algonquian *scoutiouabou* (*ishkotéwabó* in Father Baraga's Ojibwa grammar). It is difficult to say whether the many compounds with *war* (*-chief, -club, -party, -path,* etc.) are all translations of actual Indian terms. Combinations such as *maiaosé-winini,* 'war chief,' did exist in some of the languages, but no evidence exists to indicate whether the English formation is a literal translation or just an attribution or an imagined translation. Likewise, Ojibwa *wâbinêsiwin* did mean 'paleness of the face'; it may or may not have been the origin of *paleface.* Unfortunately we have little evidence of the attempts of the American Indians to speak pidgin-like English, aside from such late developments as Chinook, otherwise the origin of certain of these compounds, as well as of expressions like *Great White Father* and *bury the hatchet,* might possibly be clarified.

II. FRENCH INFLUENCE

Besides the various Indian influences, American English reflects the other non-English cultures which the colonists and frontiersmen met in their conquest of the continent. In the westward expansion of their territory, the English-speaking colonists soon came into contact with the French. Explorers, trappers, traders, and missionaries had streamed into the valleys of the St. Lawrence and the Mississippi, following hard upon the trail of Champlain and LaSalle. By 1700 the French held virtually all the strategic posts along these great rivers and a number of vital points on the shores of the Great Lakes as well.

This was the world of the *voyageurs*, the *coureurs de(s)bois*, and the *habitants*—a riotous and colorful frontier, invaded twice a year by rough, simple, and hairy woods runners, either enroute to trap the furs which were so vital to the economy of France, or returning triumphantly with their booty.

In striking contrast New Orleans, the center of French influence in this country, was for a long time the most European of American cities. It boasted a prosperous theater which catered to wealthy aristocrats from all over the South. It was this city which in 1806 introduced grand opera to America. A distinct though somewhat derivative architecture and an excellent cuisine contributed to its metropolitan atmosphere.

Thus in their sweep toward the Mississippi the English encountered two types of French culture: a very casual colonial civilization and a quite fully developed urban one. In addition, of the various languages with which the Anglo-Saxons were to come into contact, only French had a generally acknowledged prestige value. There had always been some knowledge of French among the cultivated in the English-speaking colonies. The language was important in New England because Calvin had written in it; in the South because it constituted part of the equipment of a gentleman. The influence of French thought rose to a height during the last half of the eighteenth century, with such figures as Franklin and Jefferson of paramount importance in its transmission.

The words in present-day American English which may be traced to the French in America, classified according to the aspects of life and fields of activity they represent, are as follows:

The French loan words are somewhat fewer than those from the American Indian languages, but many of the same problems present themselves in the compilation of what might be considered an authentic list. Such words as *pirogue, coulee,* and *lagniappe* are distinctly regional in their occurrence. Like the Amer-

PLANTS AND ANIMALS

caribou
crappie
gopher
pumpkin

FOODS

brioche
chowder
jambalaya *
(pie) a la mode
praline
sazarac

TOPONYMICS

bayou
butte
chute
coulee
crevasse
flume
levee
prairie
rapids
sault

FURNITURE AND BUILDING

bureau
depot
shanty

EXPLORATION AND TRAVEL

bateau
cache
carry-all
pirogue
portage
toboggan
voyageur

COINAGE

cent
dime
mill

MISCELLANEOUS

apache
(Indian) brave
Cajun
calumet
Canuck
chambray
charivari
lacrosse
lagniappe
parlay
picayune
rotisserie
sashay

* The suggestion of an African origin for this word has recently been made, but it is recorded in Modern Provençal.

ican Indian loans, many French borrowings have long since ceased to be an active part of the language. In 1902 Sylva Clapin listed as many as 102 French loan words in his *New Dictionary of Americanisms.* Although some were not French to begin with, many others, such as *bogue, bagasse,* and *cordelle,* are no longer current, and again such words as *movey star* (mauvaises terres), *coteau*, and *bob ruly* (bois brulé) would be recognized only along the Canadian border or in Cajun territory.

The French borrowings tend generally to fall into two groups. First, there are a number of words pertaining to exploration and travel, or descriptive of features of the landscape. For the most part these terms result from the contact between English and French in the central states, as undoubtedly did such miscellaneous items as *charivari* (regularly pronounced *shivaree* in the United States), *calumet*, and *lacrosse*. On the other hand, food terms like *jambalaya*, *praline*, and *sazarac* suggest the superb chefs, confectioners, and bartenders in the New Orleans area. The three coinage terms, *cent*, *dime*, and *mill*, were borrowings from continental rather than colonial French, the first citations appearing in the 1780's, when our monetary system was established largely through the instrumentality of Robert Morris.

Although French was the immediate source of all the words listed here, some of them had originated in other languages. *Bayou*, for example, was a Choctaw word *bayuk*, meaning river or creek. It developed a variety of applications in different parts of the country, depending generally upon the topography and climate. An early French citation drawn from Louisiana records reads, 'A cinq lieues plus loin, en tournant tousjours à la gauche sur le lac, on trouve une eau dormante, que les sauvages appellent Bayouque.' In Texas and the West the word means a deep inlet which affords a channel for the water in times of flood but remains dry or nearly so at other seasons. Along the Mississippi it may be used for an abandoned river course.

Caribou was likewise Indian in origin; it came from Micmac *khalibu*, 'pawer or scratcher'; *toboggan* was borrowed by the French from the same language. There has been considerable discussion concerning *lagniappe*, a common term in the South for a small gift; the most authoritative analysis of the evidence concludes that it is a Louisiana French transformation of Spanish *la ñapa*, which was possibly taken from Quechua, one of the languages indigenous to South America. *Parlay*, a term originally used in connection with gambling and horse racing, is an adaptation by the French of Italian *paroli.*

Unlike the Amerindian loan words, at least half of which came into the language during the seventeenth century, the borrowings from the French appear chiefly during the eighteenth and nineteenth centuries. It is true that *sault* is recorded as early as 1600 in one of Hakluyt's *Voyages,* but the next use of it does not appear until 1809. The earliest citation for *caribou* is 1672; that for *portage* is 1698, in an English translation of the works of Father Hennepin; and Nathaniel Ward appears to have been the first to have reworked the French *pompion* into *pumpkin* in 1647. Except for these, the French loans are divided fairly evenly between the two succeeding centuries. In this connection we must also remember that in the nineteenth century the English language in general borrowed more words from continental French than at any time after the end of the Middle Ages. These general English borrowings, however, were chiefly terms dealing with art, literature, dress, textiles, furniture, and cooking; they have a quite different flavor from the peculiarly American loan words.

In the course of the borrowing process, the French words were by no means as violently distorted in form and pronunciation as were the American Indian terms. Even though the spelling may have been considerably altered at times, as in the case of *gopher,* derived from *gaufre,* 'honeycomb,' a radical change in pronunciation is not necessarily implied. The most pronounced tendency is to stress the first syllable, or at any rate to shift it forward, as evidenced in *coulee, bureau, depot, picayune,* and many others in the list, but this has always been characteristic of the English treatment of French loan words. English does not have a sound like French *u;* consequently the stressed vowels of *butte, flume,* and *bureau* were dealt with according to English phonetic patterns.

Nor is there nearly as much deviation from the etymological meanings of the French borrowings as was true of the American Indian loan words. *Praline,* for which the earliest recorded citations are English rather than American but which has since been used chiefly in the United States, takes its name from the French marshal whose cook invented the confection. *Chowder* appears to have been taken from Breton *chaudière,* 'cauldron.' One of the most difficult etymological problems is posed by the word *shanty,* which is ascribed by some scholars to Canadian French *chantier,* 'shed for storing timber,' and by others to Irish *sean,* 'old,' and *tigh,* 'house.' The nature, place, and dates of the earliest American citations, however, seem to confirm the theory of French rather than Irish origin. The outstanding example of folk etymology among this group of words is *carryall,* a reworking of *carriole.*

The changes of meaning reflected in the French borrowings are at times more complex than those from the Amerindians partly because so many of the words represent a second borrowing of the same term. *Portage,* for example, had existed in English for several centuries in a number of meanings, some of which were archaic or obsolescent when the word was borrowed in its present highly specialized American sense. *Dime,* with the general meaning of 'one-tenth,' had come into British English as early as 1377, but it had dropped out of the language altogether prior to its revival as part of our monetary terminology.

On other occasions the American adoption of a French word has preceded an independent borrowing in England. For example, *crevasse,* which in America refers to a break in a levee, was adopted some years later in England to indicate a fissure or chasm in the ice of a glacier. This meaning was subsequently adopted in America also. The American use of *coulee,* 'a small stream or stream bed,' is first cited in 1807, more than thirty years earlier than the British borrowing in a technical geological sense, referring to a lava flow.

One of the most interesting series of semantic changes has occurred in connection with the word *depot.* This came into English late in the eighteenth century, meaning first the act of depositing, then the deposit or collection itself, and later as a term for the place where virtually anything might be deposited—

military stores, prisoners of war, or merchandise. About 1830, with the development of the railroad, the term was adopted for what the *Oxford English Dictionary* calls, 'a goods station at a terminus.' In America, however, the term was extended to freight depositories all along the line and not merely at terminal points. But also in America, particularly in the sparsely populated sections of the country where the railroad often pushed beyond actual settlement, the same small building was regularly used to store goods, sell tickets, and shelter passengers. Consequently, *depot* came to be used for a passenger station as well. There followed, then, possibly in the second decade of this century, a period in which *depot* came to be regarded as old-fashioned, if not countrified, and a good deal of effort was expended in attempting to substitute *station* in its place, often with such amusing inconsistencies as having the Pennsylvania Railroad Station located on Depot Street. Finally, with the development of cross-country and transcontinental bus travel, *depot* seems to have come into its own again as the current term for a bus passengers' waiting room. It is worth observing, however, that *depot wagon*, used as early as 1908 for a horse-drawn vehicle, became *station wagon* as a result of the decline of the prestige of *depot*; here no tendency toward the reinstatement of *depot* has been apparent.

Picayune, originally the name of a small coin, has been extended to anything trifling, and at times to the mean or contemptible. *Apache* represents a curious instance of what might be called a loan followed by repayment. The French, after experimenting with various Indian tribal names as a term for the gangsters in and about Paris, finally hit upon *Apache*, which seemed to be satisfactory. It was then taken back into both British and American English, particularly with reference to the somewhat abandoned type of dancing characteristic of the low class French halls and cafés.

Except for *sashay*, which the *Oxford English Dictionary* with rather unnecessary severity classifies as 'U.S. vulgar,' the French loan words were all borrowed as nouns. The three in particular which have attained the widest use as verbs are *portage, cache,*

and *toboggan*. With the last two the transformation was very
rapid, occurring within a quarter of a century after the adoption
of the substantive. The same rapidity of conversion may be observed in the change of *picayune* from noun to adjective.

With respect to compound formations, undoubtedly the most
prolific of the borrowed words was *prairie*, which is represented
by more than eighty combinations in *Webster*. *Gopher*, with
fourteen on record, makes a poor second. Such derivatives as
picayunish, picayunishness, tobogganer, and *tobogganist* serve to
increase the total impact of French upon American English, but
these pale into insignificance in comparison with the recent popularity of the *-ee* suffix. Particularly striking has been the tendency to apply the originally feminine form of the past participle
(*-ée*) to masculine derivatives as well. British English in general
preserves, or at least used to preserve, the niceties of both gender
and written accentuation, but in the United States an *employee*
could be either male or female from the time of the first use of
the word. The last few years have seen a host of new formations,
including *draftee, selectee, rushee, parolee, trainee*. In *conferee*,
a very early formation, and *escapee*, a recent one, the function
of the derivative ending has been altered from that of object to
subject.

III. SPANISH INFLUENCE

The Spanish colonization and culture encountered by the English-speaking settlers as they moved southward toward the Gulf
of Mexico and westward toward the Rockies and the Pacific
were more permanent and substantial than the casual French
settlements which they had found in the Middle West. Though
disappointed in their quest for gold and precious stones in this
part of the American continent, the Spaniards did establish
colonies in which the large individual haciendas subsisted as
independent units. This hacienda culture, commonly encountered
in Mexico as recently as the first decade of the present century,

was characteristic of Texas and the Southwest when in 1806 Zebulon Pike attempted the ascent of the peak which bears his name, when Stephen Austin and Samuel Houston moved into the Lone Star State, and when the intrepid 'forty-niners crowded into California in their frenzied search for gold.

The words still common in American English which may be traced to the Spanish in America, classified according to the aspects of life and fields of activity they represent, are as follows:

PLANTS AND ANIMALS

alfalfa	chigger (jigger)	
marijuana	cockroach	
mesquite	coyote	
yucca	mustang	
armadillo	palomino	
bronco	pinto	
burro	vinegarroon	
barracuda		
bonito		
pompano		

RANCH LIFE

buckaroo	peon
chaparral	quirt
cinch	ranch
corral	reata
cuarta	rodeo
hacienda	stampede
lariat	wrangler
lasso	

FOOD AND DRINK

chile con carne
enchilada
frijole
jerk (jerked meat)
mescal
pinion nuts
taco
tamale
tequila
tortilla

BUILDING

adobe
cafeteria
patio
plaza
pueblo

MINING

bonanza
placer

CLOTHING

chaps
poncho
serape
sombrero
ten-gallon hat

LEGAL AND PENAL

calaboose
cuartel
desperado
hoosegow
incommunicado
vigilantes

TOPONYMICS

   arroyo
   barranca
   canyon
   key
   mesa
   sierra

RACES AND NATIONALITIES

   conch
   coon
   creole
   dago
   mulatto
   octoroon
   pickaninny
   quadroon

MISCELLANEOUS

   coquina
   fiesta
   filibuster
   hombre
   loco
   marina
   mosey
   pronto
   rumba
   savvy
   stevedore
   temblor
   tornado
   vamoose

The eighty-odd terms listed here, though certainly not all-inclusive, are greater in number than either the borrowings from the various Indian languages or those from the French. And here again is the problem of what to include and what to omit. Certain words, such as *taco* and *frijole,* are better known along the Mexican border than elsewhere. Others like *reata* and *palomino* are widely current only in the Far West, whereas some fish names, notably *pompano,* are characteristic chiefly of the Gulf Coast. The *Dictionary of Spanish Terms in English,* compiled by Dr. Harold Bentley, lists about 400 borrowings in all, and Dr. Ralph W. Sorvig has more than doubled this number in his study of loan words from just the American Southwest. But these include such terms as *alcalde* and *cuartel,* likely to be used only in the completely Hispanized sections of New Mexico and Texas, or in California. Even many of the 156 Spanish loan words to be found in Sylva Clapin's *Dictionary of Americanisms* would scarcely be known to the general reader living some distance north of the early Spanish settlements.

Still another difficulty arises in connection with certain words. Although such terms as *alligator, avocado, banana, palmetto,* and *potato* were originally Spanish-American in origin, they have become current in British as well as American English. This is also true of such originally indigenous words as *chocolate* and *tapioca*, the latter in fact having come into English through Portuguese. It is scarcely justifiable, therefore, to consider these as peculiarly American.

It is immediately obvious that the largest group of adoptions from the Spanish reflects the hacienda culture which typified the Spanish colonial occupation and the ranching and mining economies which developed out of it. The buildings, the occupations, the clothing, and even the legal and penal systems of ranch life are reflected here. There are more plant, animal, and fish names than from the French, but they are not as numerous as Indian loan words in the same category. Words indicating features of the topography are fewer in number than those from the French, and there are no terms dealing with exploration and travel. It is interesting to observe how many of our terms, both serious and jocular, for various races and nationalities are drawn from Spanish.

As with the French loan words, there is evidence of Spanish borrowing from the languages of the various Indian nations with which they came into contact, prior to the adoption of these words into English. *Coyote* was taken by the Spaniards from Aztec or Nahuatl *coyotl*. *Tequila* may even have been a Nahuatl borrowing from some other Indian language, and *jerk*, 'to preserve,' as it occurs in *jerked meat* reflects a Spanish *charquear*, *charqui*, taken from one of the Peruvian Indian languages. The precise path of transmission of *pickaninny* is not absolutely clear; it may represent an African adaptation of Portuguese *pequenino* rather than Spanish *pequeño niño*. *Rumba* was originally of African origin, and *filibuster* reflects a Spanish *filibustero*, which had in turn been taken by way of French from Dutch *vrijbuiter*, 'freebooter.'

In contrast both to the Indian loan words, which were numerous in our early history and progressively died out as time went on, and to the French adoptions, which have gradually increased with the centuries, borrowing from the Spanish was heavy during the seventeenth and nineteenth centuries and considerably lighter in the eighteenth. Plant and animal names and words for races and nationalities appear early. Prominent among the first adoptions are such words as *tomato, barbecue, savannah, chocolate,* and *sarsaparilla,* which became equally common in Britain and America and consequently were not included in the foregoing listing. In contrast, the ranching, mining, and building terms did not appear for the most part until the last century, and those reflecting the Mexican cuisine are of even more recent adoption.

The majority of these borrowings continue to end in *a* and *o* in English as they did in Spanish—although *ranch, cinch, quirt,* and *filibuster* are notable exceptions—and since the five distinctive vowels of Spanish are all present in English, there was nothing that occasioned radical changes in form or pronunciation. Certain of the Spanish loans do display somewhat more pronounced alterations, involving particularly the consonant sounds. For example, Spanish *juzgado,* the past participle of the verb 'to judge,' came to mean first a court of justice and, in Mexico, a jail. Initial *j* in Spanish is pronounced like a somewhat constricted English *h.* In many varieties of Spanish, *d* in the suffix *-ado* virtually disappears, leaving the vowel combination *-ao,* which sounds not too unlike *ow* in English *cow.* Only when all these factors are taken into account can the transformation of *juzgado* to English *hoosegow* be comprehended. Equally striking are such developments as *buckaroo* from *vaquero, wrangler* from *caballerango,* and *mustang* from *mesteño.*

A few Spanish loans have given rise to two words in English. In *lariat* and *reata* the first includes and the second omits the definite article. *Vamoose* and *mosey* are both from Spanish *vamos,* a form of the verb 'to go.' As is generally true with borrowings from any of the Romance languages, English tends to shift the stress forward. This is illustrated by *stevedore* from *estivadór, canyon* from *cañón, cannibal* from *canibál,* to mention only a few.

No striking deviations from etymological meaning are to be

found among these words, although *dago* was presumably derived from the proper name *Diego,* the Spanish equivalent of James. The most picturesque development among all the Spanish borrowings is again an instance of folk or popular etymology. The Spanish word for braid is *galón.* It appears that the wide-brimmed hats worn by cowboys and ranchers were originally decorated with a number of braids at the base of the crown, from which the expression *ten-* (or *five*) *gallon hat* was derived, which was mistakenly interpreted as a reference to its potential liquid capacity. Beside this, *cockroach,* another attempt to break up a strange word (*cucaracha*) into meaningful elements, appears as a rather insipid display of the imagination.

Among the words presenting the most extensive and complex series of meaning changes is *creole.* In the Spanish colonies *criollo* was a term applied to someone born in the region but of European, usually Spanish, ancestry. Naturally enough the word had this meaning in Louisiana when that territory passed from Spanish to French control. The word was taken over by the French and in its French form came to be used for a person born in Louisiana, but of French ancestry. After the American occupation of the area, the term was applied to the dialect of French spoken there, to those who spoke it—consequently at times to persons of mixed French and Negro ancestry—to native-born as distinguished from African-born Negroes, to a sauce typical of the cookery of the region. All of this a far cry from the original verb which meant 'to create or bring up.'

Some of the concomitant aspects of word borrowing have been discussed in sufficient detail in connection with the Indian and the French loan words so that they need only brief mention here. Again most of the Spanish borrowings are nouns, although the adjective *loco,* the adverb *pronto,* and the verbs *vamoose, mosey,* and *savvy* do demonstrate for the first time an influence somewhat deeper than the casual substantive level. Such nouns as *stampede, lasso, ranch, barbecue,* and the hybrids *filibuster* and *jerk* quite readily developed into verbs. *Ranch* has given rise to about a dozen compound forms, and no less than twenty compounds peculiar to American usage have been formed from the noun *mosquito,* even though the word itself appears at times in British as well as in American English.

The most interesting combinative development is to be seen in connection with *cafeteria.* Just how it came into the English language is not known in full detail. The earliest recorded dictionary citation is 1918, but the word appears to have been used at least ten years earlier in California in something like its present sense, and considerably before that in Chicago. Its Spanish equivalent was recorded in a dictionary of Cuban Spanish published in 1862.

In Spanish, *-ería* was and is still a highly productive suffix, as a ten-minute walk through any Spanish-speaking city or village will clearly demonstrate. The main street will be lined with signs bearing such legends as *carnicería, ferretería, planchadería, tintorería, carpintería, abarrotería*—and as one approaches the United States border, even *droguería* and *lonchería. Cafetería* was merely another formation of this type. The mid-nineteenth century records of its use in Cuba and Mexico show it to have been applied to a small restaurant serving ordinary alcoholic drinks and plain meals. From here it seems to have spread to the Spanish-speaking residents of California, but as a place for drinking rather than eating. Then, during the last decade of the nineteenth century, some enterprising restaurateur, probably seeking a novel and arresting name for his establishment, seized upon the word. Whether the first American cafeteria dispensed with waiters is not known, but in due course the self-service feature became implicit in the term. Since the word *café* was already commonly used for a restaurant in which table service was supplied, it was natural that the suffix *-teria,* derived by subtraction, so to speak, came to be connected with the idea of self-service. By natural extension *groceteria, bookateria, snacketeria,* and *hardware-ateria* came into being for other types of businesses in which the customer waited upon himself. Ultimately we find such bizarre creations as *shaveteria, smoketeria, valeteria,* and *bobateria* where the self-service idea does not apply. In all, there have been at least forty derivatives from this single suffix.

IV. DUTCH INFLUENCE

Long before their drive westward had penetrated into the realm of the French voyageurs and habitants and the Spanish *haciendados*, the aggressive English colonists had dispossessed another European nation of its North American territory. The country was Holland; the industrious burghers and powerful patroons of New Amsterdam became a part of the English colonial empire in 1664.

Even during its short existence as part of the far-flung empire of the House of Orange, the compact settlement in the Hudson Valley had developed a mode of life and a culture quite its own, as the following description of life in a Dutch household suggests.

As to the family, they always entered in at the gate, and most generally lived in the kitchen. To have seen a numerous household assembled around the fire, one would have imagined that he was transported back to those happy days of primeval simplicity, which float before our imaginations like golden visions. The fireplaces were of a truly patriarchal magnitude, where the whole family, old and young, master and servant, black and white, nay even the very cat and dog, enjoyed a community of privilege, and had each a prescriptive right to a corner. Here the old burgher would sit in perfect silence, puffing his pipe, looking in the fire with half shut eyes, and thinking of nothing for hours together; the goede vrouw on the opposite side would employ herself diligently in spinning her yarn, or knitting stockings. The young folks would crowd around the hearth; listening with breathless attention to some old crone of a negro, who was the oracle of the family,—and who, perched like a raven in a corner of the chimney, would croak forth for a long winter afternoon, a string of incredible stories about New England witches—grisly ghosts—horses without heads—and hairbreadth escapes and bloody encounters among the Indians.

This was the world of Walter the Doubter, William the Testy, and hard-headed Peter Stuyvesant, immortalized by Washington Irving in his *Knickerbocker History*. Caricature though his account may be, Irving does give us a picture of the general culture of the area. It was only natural that some evidences of this way of life ultimately came to be reflected in the language of the English-speaking colonists who came into contact with it. The words in American English which are of Dutch origin or show other evidences of Dutch influence, classified according to the aspects of life and fields of activity they represent, are as follows:

FOOD

cole slaw
cookie
cruller
pit ('stone' or 'seed')
pot cheese
waffle

TOPONYMICS

bush ('back country')
hook (of land)

TRANSPORTATION

caboose
scow
sleigh
span (of horses)

FARM AND BUILDING

hay barrack
stoop ('porch')
saw buck

SOCIAL CLASSIFICATION

boss
patroon
Yankee

MISCELLANEOUS

boodle
dingus
dope
dumb ('stupid')
logy
poppycock
Santa Claus
snoop
spook

Although only twenty-seven words appear in the list, they are in much more general use than either the Spanish or the French loan words. They form a part of the most intimate fabric of the language. Six of them pertain to foods, but aside from these there are few which represent any particular class of idea or sphere of activity.

Some of the terms are wholly or in part loan translations rather than direct appropriations from the Dutch lexicon. *Pot cheese* is modeled on Dutch *pot kees*. *Saw buck* could have been formed either on the basis of Dutch *zaagbock* or German *Sägebock*; quite possibly both languages had a hand in establishing it in this country. At least twenty different etymologies have been proposed for that most typically American of all words, *Yankee*, but among these the most credible seems to be Dutch *Jan Kees*, 'John Cheese,' a term applied to the New Englanders somewhat contemptuously, or at least patronizingly. This was mistaken for a plural by the English-speaking colonists and a new singular, *Yankee*, was derived through the process of back-formation.

Since contact with the Dutch colonists was established during the seventeenth century, it is not surprising to find dictionary citations for approximately one-third of the Dutch loan words bearing dates prior to 1800. The earliest words to appear in American English were *scow* in 1660, *sleigh* in 1703, *patroon* in 1744, *caboose* in 1747, *stoop* in 1755, *span* in 1769. Most of the remaining words are found sometime during the first part of the nineteenth century. This is important, for it definitely marks the original settlement in New York as the place of origin of the Dutch borrowings rather than such later colonies as that of the Van Raalte group, which settled in western Michigan in the 1840's, or the subsequent settlements in Wisconsin and Iowa. Moreover, a number of terms of Dutch origin, such as *erve*, 'small inheritance,' *kolf baan*, 'mall for a game played with mallet and ball,' and *rolliche*, 'meat roulade,' once current in the Hudson Valley, are either entirely obsolete or are disappearing rapidly.

Of all the languages which have made a significant contribution to the American lexicon, Dutch is most closely related to English. Consequently there are fewer changes in form and pronunciation in the Dutch borrowings than in those from somewhat more remote and differently constructed languages. A good many of the words now spelled with *oo,* some of which are pronounced with the vowel of *food,* were spelled *oe* in Dutch and pronounced with the vowel of *pull.* This was true of *hoek, snoepen,* and *stoep,* corresponding to English *hook, snoop,* and *stoop,* respectively. *Claus,* in Santa Claus developed from a Dutch *sinterklaas,* a somewhat collapsed form of Sant Nikolaas. However, since American English of the late eighteenth century did not have the [ɑ] vowel of *father,* the [ɔ] vowel, as in *log,* developed as the closest approximation. This is also true of *boss* (Du. *baas*).

Undoubtedly the word *caboose* presents the most unusual example of a change from its original meaning. At the outset it was used with reference to a ship's galley, and is still so employed in Great Britain. Subsequent American meanings, however, include that of outdoor oven (1786), hut (1839), and finally its present meaning of a car serving as the headquarters for a freight train crew. The earliest citations for this meaning have *caboose car. Caboose* used by itself with reference to railroading is first quoted in 1871.

A comment by James Fenimore Cooper on the word *boss* affords an excellent illustration of at least one motive for word borrowing. In a section on language in *The American Democrat* (1838) he remarks:

> In consequence of the domestic servants of America having once been negro slaves, a prejudice has arisen among the laboring classes of the whites, who not only dislike the term *servant,* but have also rejected that of *master.* So far has this prejudice gone, that in lieu of the latter, they have resorted to the use of the word *boss,* which has precisely the same meaning in Dutch! How far a subterfuge of this nature is worthy of a manly and common sense people, will admit of question.

We must also recognize that a number of words took only one meaning from the language of the Low Countries, but have other meanings which already existed in English. This is true, for example of *pit,* in the sense of the hard kernel of a peach or cherry. It is only this one particular use which was borrowed from Dutch; other meanings of this extremely familiar word were already common to both languages. Other instances of the same process include *bush,* with the meaning of back country, *stoop* for porch, and *span* used with reference to horses. It should be observed that the distribution of some of these meanings, such as *pit* and *stoop,* as well as of certain whole word borrowings, is distinctly regional. *Hay barrack* is definitely confined to the Hudson Valley, and *pot cheese* is limited to a slightly larger area which includes eastern Pennsylvania and northern New Jersey as well.

Except for the adjectives *dumb* and *logy* and the verb *snoop,* most of the Dutch loan words were borrowed as nouns, but they lent themselves easily to change of function. *Pit, boss,* and *sleigh* were all changed into verbs. *Boodle,* perhaps, presents the outstanding illustration of the tendency to form derivatives. The *Oxford English Dictionary* lists *boodleize, boodleism, boodleistic, boodler, boodlerism,* and *boodling,* and the *Dictionary of American English* adds *boodlery* to the list.

V. GERMAN INFLUENCE

The German element in the vocabulary of American English is the first, among those considered, to stem from an immigrant people, not a conquered colonial rival. This gives a somewhat new turn to the word-borrowing process.

The German migrations to America consist of three or four major waves. As early as 1683, immigrants from the southwestern part of Germany had begun to settle in Pennsylvania. By 1775 they numbered about 90,000, largely from the Rhenish Palatinate. These Germans developed a language consisting of a compromise of their own various dialects with a strong admixture of English words and constructions. We have come to know and refer to this as Pennsylvania Dutch. Though dying out more rapidly now than in former times, it is still spoken by at least 25 per cent of the inhabitants of Lehigh, Lebanon, and Berks counties in Pennsylvania, and understood by from 60 to 65 per cent. Its extraordinary persistence is due to the clannishness of the Pennsylvania Germans, based in part upon the religious separatism evident in such sects as the Amish and the Mennonites.

The second wave of German migration began as early as 1830, but reached its crest in 1849, after the collapse of the liberal movement in the fatherland, when such patriots as Carl Schurz came to this country. Although many German rural communities sprang up as a result of the movement, much of the settlement was metropolitan. In Milwaukee, Chicago, Cleveland, Cincinnati, St. Louis, Detroit, Buffalo, and New York, Germans were gathered together in groups large enough to maintain their own language and cultural traditions for a considerable length of time. German-language dailies flourished in all the large cities of the Middle West until 1917. The Germans had their own schools as well, and they maintained strong church and fraternal organizations. Subsequent large-scale movements in the 'eighties of the last century and early in the present century tended to maintain the traditions of the fatherland for a considerable period of time. Despite the curtailment of immigration under the quota system after the First World War, the Germans still constitute the largest body of non-English speaking stock in the United States.

The words in American English which are of German origin or show some aspects of German influence, classified according to the aspects of life and fields of activity they represent, are:

FOOD AND DRINK	FOOD AND DRINK
beer soup	lager beer
blutwurst	liverwurst
bock beer	noodle
delicatessen	ponhaus
dunk	pretzel
fossnocks	pumpernickel
frankfurter	sauerbraten
hamburger	sauerkraut

FOOD AND DRINK

schnitzel
smear case
snits
springerle
stollen
sweitzer cheese
thick milk
wienerwurst
zwieback

EDUCATIONAL

diener ('laboratory assistant')
festschrift
semester
seminar

SOCIAL

Belschnickel
beer garden
bower ('jack' or 'knave')
Christmas tree

SOCIAL

Kris Kringle
pinochle
poker *
rathskeller
saengerfest
stein
Turner
turnverein

MISCELLANEOUS

bub
bum
fresh ('impudent')
hausfrau
hex (noun and verb)
katzenjammer
loafer
nix
ouch
phooey
spiel, spieler
wunderkind

* A French origin for this word has also been suggested.

The loan words listed here are about fifty in number, but again there is the difficulty of knowing what to include and what to omit. Should *turnverein* be considered in current use, or are the gymnastic, literary, and recreational organizations founded through the impetus given by Vater Jahn now completely a dead letter in American life? Or if *turnverein* is obsolescent, how about *Turners*, or *Turner Hall*, which may linger on somewhat more tenaciously? And the *saengerfeste*, though not as numerous as they once were, still survive in various parts of the country, as for example the region around New Braunfels in Texas, where as many as 5000 may be present at these gatherings.

Then there is the problem of such compounds as *rainworm*, *cookbook*, and *back country*, which may be explained as transla-

tions of *Regenwurm, Kockbuch,* and *Hinterland* respectively;
but they could conceivably have arisen as purely native developments. Even Superman, that truly unique product of modern
comic-book culture, might be reckoned to have his origin in
either Shaw or Nietzsche. There are also such regionalisms as
ponhaws, 'scrapple,' *fossnocks,* 'doughnuts,' and *Belschnickel,*
'Santa Claus,' current chiefly in the Pennsylvania Dutch and
derivative areas.

Despite these difficulties, a glance at the categories listed on
the preceding pages does give us an idea of the cultural contact
between German immigrants and their English-speaking hosts.
There can be little doubt that a considerable portion of this contact centered about the dining-room table, the free-lunch counter,
and the tavern bar. There is a decided persistence of food terms
and words reflecting pleasant but commonplace social contacts.
In contrast, the educational terms reflect not so much the German migration to America as the nineteenth-century practice of
American educators and professional men in going to Germany
for postgraduate study. The impact of this upon the American
educational system is, in fact, considerably more profound than
these few terms indicate, for it includes such features as the
elective system of courses, the ideal of academic freedom, and
the current concept of study leading to the doctorate.

In general, the German borrowings came into English during
the nineteenth century. Although both *noodle,* first cited by the
Dictionary of American English in 1812, and *sauerkraut,* in 1813,
seem to have been used in England considerably earlier, there is
every reason to believe that the American use of these words
represents an independent borrowing. These, along with *Belschnickel* in 1823, *smear case* in 1829, *Kris Kringle* in 1830, *loafer*
in 1835, *poker* in 1836, and *ouch* in 1839, must have come from
Pennsylvania or its derivative settlements. They are certainly
too early for the nineteenth-century migration centering about
the 'forty-eighters to have taken effect. The earliest citation dates
for the remaining words are distributed fairly evenly throughout
the century. Even such commonplaces of present-day American

life as *pretzel, hamburger,* and *frankfurter* do not put in their appearance until 1874, 1884, and 1899 respectively. In general the German borrowings have been nouns, but it is of some interest to observe such interjections as *nix, ouch,* and *phooey* among them, and at least one scholar assumes *hurrah* to have been an early importation from the German as well. Words of this nature bespeak something deeper than the most casual linguistic intercourse.

Probably the most productive word-forming elements accruing from this contact with the German language are the prefix *ker-* and the suffixes *-fest* and *-burger.* The first of these, undoubtedly traceable to the German past-participle prefix *ge-,* appears chiefly in such colloquial combinations as *kerflop, kerplunk, kersmash.* We find *-fest* in *gabfest, talkfest, swatfest,* and *slugfest.* It is *-burger,* however, which presents by far the most interesting series of developments.

A number of German food terms adopted in this country have geographical designations. *Frankfurter, wienerwurst,* and even the more recent *braunschweiger* and *thüringer* are all instances of sausages labeled in terms of their presumed place of origin. *Hamburger steak,* a designation first appearing in 1884, is but a further extension of this same tendency. We find this shortened to *hamburger* by 1901. The next stage in our story of the *-burger* suffix must have been the development of the now typical hamburger sandwich, fried ground beef served in a round roll or bun. At this point the process of folk etymology begins to operate. The meat itself was equated with the element *ham,* understandably enough though scarcely accurate, and *-burger* came to denote what surrounded it. Consequently, as the filling element of the sandwich varied, so did the first element of the combination, and within a short space of time, lunch counter and drive-in restaurant menus began to feature *cheeseburgers, chickenburgers, turkeyburgers, lamburgers, ham-and-egg burgers, riceburgers, fishburgers, shrimpburgers,* and at one time when a presidential suggestion attempted to put into practice an unpopular meat-saving scheme, even a *Trumanburger.*

An interesting group of borrowings related to, or really an extension of, the German loan words are those which have Yiddish as their source. Except for *kosher* and *kibitzer,* and the somewhat outdated slang *mazuma* for money, they have not passed into American English generally. But certainly many people in the metropolitan centers, irrespective of their background, can identify *mishuggah, schlemihl, schnookel, schickse, gefüllte fish,* and possibly *schlepper* and *schnorer.*

Other immigrant stocks have also enriched the English of America but not in such quantity. From the various African languages spoken by those who were imported as slaves come such terms as *gumbo, goober, buckra, juba, voodoo,* and *hoodoo.* The recently popularized *juke,* as in *juke joint* and *juke box* is thought to have had a similar history. In the dialect known as Gullah, spoken by Negroes living on the islands off the coasts of North Carolina, South Carolina, and Georgia, it has been estimated that as many as 6000 African words are still current.

In addition, languages as widely varied as Swedish, Italian, and Chinese have all made some contributions to the American vocabulary. Owing to the numbers of Scandinavian restaurants which have become established throughout the country, the institution of the *smörgasbord* is familiar to millions of Americans, and *lutfisk* is well known in those regions originally settled by the Swedes and Norwegians. *Skijor* and *skijoring* are also in current use. Judging from its omission from the body proper of the *Oxford English Dictionary, spaghetti* may be a more common term in America than in England, though it is certainly used in both countries. It appears to be to the Italians also that we owe the terms *policy-ticket* (now generally replaced by *numbers* in this and certain other compounds), *ravioli, minestrone,* and *black-hand. Antipasto,* not recorded in the *Oxford English Dictionary,* does appear in *Webster's,* and without question *pizza* and *pizzeria* have recently shown marked gains in currency here. From Chinese (or pidgin English) we have adopted *chow, chowmein, chop suey, fantan,* and *joss.*

In fact, almost every region of the United States heavily peopled by some one immigrant stock has borrowed a number of words from the foreign language in question, words which generally have a fairly limited local currency. Thus in the northern peninsula of Michigan, with large numbers of people of Finnish extraction, the term *sauna* for steam bath is in common use. *Cush* for a pancake made of cornmeal, and *cala*, a rice cake, both of African origin, are well known in sections of the country heavily populated by Negroes.

Examples could be multiplied indefinitely, but hasty and tentative as this discussion of loan words has been, enough has been said to demonstrate that the kinds of words the Americans have borrowed from other languages are not the result of mere whim or chance, but contrariwise, that they bear eloquent testimony to the nature of our contact with the culture which each of those languages represents. 'Milestones of general history,' is how the Danish scholar Jespersen once characterized loan words, for, as he said, 'they show the course of civilization and the wandering of inventions and institutions, and in many cases give us valuable information as to the inner life of nations.' If rightly interpreted, he concludes, loan words will inform us of the reciprocal relations of peoples.

This chapter has attempted to demonstrate, as well, that there is considerably more to the process of word borrowing than mere addition to the vocabulary; that changes in meaning after the word is taken over, changes in grammatical function, the formation of new combinations, and the isolation of productive word-forming elements are all a part of the process.

At the turn of the present century, Israel Zangwill applied the term *melting pot* to the America which was fast becoming a complex of many old-world cultures. Long before this, Hector St. John Crèvecœur had recognized that 'here individuals of all nations are melted into a new race of men.' The millions of immigrants from Scandinavia to the Balkans, from the Indies, the Orient, and the Dark Continent, though in the main conforming to the new ways of life which they found here, could not help leaving some impress upon the heterogeneous mixture of which they formed a part. In the realm of language, it is fair to say, in precisely the same fashion, the acquisitiveness of the American vocabulary in drawing upon these many component elements of our culture, makes of American English a linguistic melting pot in miniature.

4

The Colonial Lag

So far we have considered the words which came into the English language as a result of its extension to the new world. These words had not been in the language before. They can be accounted for chiefly in terms of the particular national and racial contacts and the geographic and social environment peculiar to America. But that is only part of the story of American English.

We must remind ourselves again of two important facts: first, that the colonists who crossed the ocean in the seventeenth century were speaking the language current in the England of their day; and second, that languages change from generation to generation, but not always in the same way in various places where the language is spoken. The borrowings discussed in the preceding chapter changed the American form of the language, whereas the English variety remained comparatively unaltered with respect to these particular items. But the reverse is equally possible. Upon occasion the descendants of the early settlers might have retained words, pronunciations, forms, and modes of expression brought from England and continued in use by their elders, while in the old country these either had been dropped from use or were rapidly coming to be considered old-fashioned.

This very feature of the language in America was largely responsible for the compilation of the *Dictionary of American Eng-*

lish. Sir William Craigie, the original editor of this four-volume work, gives the following account of its inception:

> . . . one day in the Summer of 1924, in Chicago, while I was reading some proofs of the Oxford English Dictionary, I observed that in the case of two or three words beginning with the prefix *un-* the older quotations [from the Seventeenth Century] were from English sources, while the later [of the Eighteenth Century] were all American. From the evidence it seemed probable that the use of the words had continued later in this country than at home. It then occurred to me that it would be interesting to know how far back the words could be traced in American use; and that thought immediately brought me up against the fact that we had no means of ascertaining this point, for the simple reason that no effort had yet been made to trace the whole vocabulary which had been in use on this side of the ocean from the Seventeenth Century to the present day. It was then a simple matter to draw the natural conclusion that what was required was a new dictionary.

The idea that American English contains archaic features of the language which have disappeared in England itself is by no means new. As early as 1850 the second edition of J. O. Halliwell's *Dictionary of Archaisms and Provincialisms* included words 'now obsolete in England, all of which are familiar and in common use in America.' About 300 of these were included in the dictionary. The same idea is implicit in the somewhat ironic statement by James Russell Lowell that the Americans 'unhappily could bring over no English better than Shakespeare's.'

Unfortunately, the proponents of the notion of archaism in American English are often vague and superficial in their expositions of it. On an average of once every five years some well-meaning amateur in the field of folklore or cultural history 'discovers' that either the Kentucky or the Virginian or the Ozark mountaineers or members of some relatively isolated group speak the undefiled English of Chaucer or Shakespeare. The evidence adduced usually runs to such stereotyped examples as *ax* for *ask,* *hit* for *it, mought* for *might, bigged* for 'to get with child.' Actually there is an archaic element pervading all of American English, but at the same time it is quite wrong to suppose that any form of American English regional or otherwise, has preserved the language of the fourteenth or the sixteenth century without any change whatsoever. What is important is to describe this archaic element as precisely as possible and to see what forces operated to preserve it.

Again we start with the vocabulary. *Loan,* used as a transitive verb, is labeled an Americanism in most dictionaries. British usage prefers *lend.* Verbal *loan* originated in England, perhaps as early as 1200, although the earliest examples are somewhat doubtful. There is no question, however, about the authenticity of *lonyng* as it appears in the state papers of Henry VIII, and two seventeenth-century citations recorded by the *Oxford English Dictionary* are equally unmistakable. American writings employ *loan* in a verbal function as early as 1729, and indeed all of the *Oxford English Dictionary* citations for the eighteenth century are drawn from American sources. For the nineteenth and twentieth centuries, American writers continue to furnish the bulk of evidence for its use, and the 1864 edition of Webster seems to have been the first dictionary to record it.

Greenhorn gives just a slightly different twist to the archaizing process. In the sense of a novice or raw, inexperienced person, the word is not unknown in England but nevertheless is considerably more common in America. The *Oxford English Dictionary* records British citations illustrating this meaning from 1682 on, but whether by accident or design, none later than 1806. A 1790 citation is drawn from a book dealing with the West Indies. The nineteenth-century quotations are all from American authors, including Washington Irving and Horace Greeley. These data would seem to justify the conclusion that the word jumped not merely from England to the American mainland but probably to the overseas colonies generally, and that it continued in active use in this country.

Another convenient sketch of the same tendency, but this time with a significant addendum, is presented by the *Oxford English Dictionary* on the verb *to progress.* We are told here that the

word was common in England from 1590 to 1670, that it became
obsolete in England in the eighteenth century but was apparently
retained in America, where it became very common toward the
end of the century. It was readopted in England after 1800 but
often characterized there as an Americanism, and it is still much
more used in the United States. Evidence of the mid-nineteenth
century status of the word in England is furnished by the following quotation from Mary Russell Mitford: 'In country towns . . .
society has been progressing (if I may borrow that expressive
Americanism) at a very slow rate.'

This is the basic pattern which characterizes dozens of so-
called archaisms in American English. The particular words be-
having in this fashion cannot always be accounted for, but there
are certain circumstances in which such a development is likely
to take place. First of all, there are situations where British English appears to have acquired two synonymous words for the
thing or idea at about the time of our earliest colonial settlement.
One striking illustration of this is afforded by the English equiva-
lents for what we in America call a bedbug. First of all, the word
bug, originally signifying in England, as it now does in America,
an insect of any kind, specialized in meaning and came to be
applied only to the offensive little creatures found chiefly in beds
and bedsteads. The earliest citation of this special use is 1622.

At almost precisely the same time, English borrowed the word
chinch from the Spanish *chinche*, 'bedbug.' Thus, throughout the
seventeenth century, *chinch* and *bug* were synonymous in England. After 1700 *chinch* appears scarcely at all in the mother
country, but there are increasing indications of its use overseas.
A citation dated 1730 suggests that the term is used by Negroes.
There is evidence of it in Jamaica in 1756. Of the two nineteenth-
century citations in the *Oxford English Dictionary*, one is American; the other is British, but it refers to 'the impolite animal
which the transatlantics delicately designate a "chintz."' Of two
synonymous words in existence when American settlement began,
bug remained current in England; *chinch* became archaic. Since
the earlier general meaning of *bug* had been brought to America

by the first colonists, *chinch* continued in use there for a considerable time as the word for bedbug, and in fact *cinch-bug* is still widely current. As with *greenhorn,* the evidence is not confined to the American mainland but includes the West Indian settlements as well.

The word *andiron* seems to tell much the same story. There is evidence of its use in England from 1300 on. But late in the sixteenth century (1596) the compound *firedogs* also came to be applied to the same article and has continued in use down to the present. Mrs. Piozzi still used *andirons* in 1789, but in 1826 Sir Walter Scott felt it necessary to write, 'The andirons *or dogs*—for retaining the blazing firewood on the hearth.' Subsequent quotations in the *Oxford English Dictionary* are American. *Firedogs* is used in some regions of the United States, but certainly the more common *andirons* must have been brought to this country at a time when the two words were equally current in England.

At other times the creation or acceptance of a new term in England well after the beginnings of colonization resulted in the displacement of an older word in the mother country which, however, continued in use in America. This may be illustrated by *druggist.* In the early seventeenth century this term replaced the older *apothecary* which had acquired a somewhat unfavorable meaning. It was used in England as the principal term for a retail seller of medicinal drugs throughout the seventeenth century and the first half of the eighteenth century; it spread also to Scotland and the American colonies. But about 1750 or slightly before, in England itself, either a desire for elegance or for more precise definition appears to have extended the meaning of *chemist* to apply to a retail drug merchant. This extension was so complete that by 1800 *druggist* had virtually disappeared from popular usage, though retained in the combination *chemist-and-druggist* by the terms of various licensing acts. In America and Scotland the older *druggist* simply continued in use.

Frequently, too, the archaic survivals in America, though not current in standard British English, may be found still firmly entrenched in the English local or regional dialects. For example, with reference to the compound *cordwood,* the *Oxford English Dictionary* comments, 'now chiefly in America,' suggesting at least some currency throughout England at an early period. However, the only English citations are one for 1638–9 from the *North Riding Records,* another from a Kentish gloss of 1887, and a third from the 1763 volume of the *British Magazine,* but used with reference to America. The picture which thus emerges is one of regional use in seventeenth-century England, transportation to America where it became a common term, and possibly a weak extension to eighteenth-century standard British English, but certainly one which did not survive for any considerable period.

The case for *shoat,* 'a young weaned pig,' as a word once current in standard British English use is even clearer. Citations, in evidence as early as 1413, are especially numerous throughout the seventeenth century. They continue through 1722. Those appearing for the late eighteenth and early nineteenth centuries, however, are ascribed to Norfolk and Wiltshire respectively. Meanwhile the word was carried to America and has continued in use in the United States down to the present day. *Deck* for a pack of cards, apparently in common use throughout England in the sixteenth century, survives in England only in the northern dialects but is the normal term in the United States.

Similarly, *cater-cornered* is cited only for Shropshire and Leicester, and other uses of *cater-* as a compounding element are also confined to local dialects. *Drool,* used in America by Thoreau in 1854, appears to be a Somerset word; *squirt,* employed as a personal appellative, is cited from Cheshire; *pond* for a natural, not an artificial, body of water is so employed in Surrey. *Polliwog* seems to have been current throughout England until the middle of the seventeenth century; since then it has receded to the East Anglian and northern counties, although it is widely used in the United States.

The dictionary treatment of the verb *wilt* reveals a fascinating instance of a word originating in the English regional dialects, then having wide adoption in the United States, and subsequently

spreading to the standard language in England. Applied originally to plants, it developed in the English north-country, as
evidenced by Ray's dialect collection of 1691. It jumped the ocean
in the course of the eighteenth century and developed a figurative or transferred meaning in America: 'to become limp, to lose
energy or vigor.' Nineteenth-century American writers employing
the term include Timothy Dwight, Irving, Lowell, and John
Neal. At the very close of the century it was again picked up by
a British writer and in 1920 appears in the *Times Literary Sup-
plement.*

If we remember that during the seventeenth and early eighteenth centuries the English regional dialects were in a much
stronger position than they are today, and that a fair proportion
of the American settlers were speaking these dialects when they
took up land on the North American continent, it is not at all
surprising that the American vocabulary should retain in common
use a considerable number of English dialect words which are
not part of the frequently employed word stock of standard
British English.

Often it is not necessarily the whole word but an archaic or
older meaning which survives in American usage, where as in
British English subsequent semantic developments have occurred. We have already seen this to be true of *bug,* for which
American English preserves the early general meaning, whereas
the specialized significance 'bedbug' prevails in England today.
A similar development may be observed in connection with the
word *sick.* H. W. Fowler, in his *Dictionary of Modern English
Usage,* treating the status of the term in England, points out that,
'The original and more general sense of *sick,* which has now
been transferred for the most part to *ill,* was suffering from any
bodily disorder. That sense remains to it in attributive use (*sick
people, a sick child,* etc.), but is now uncommon in predicative
use (*be, feel sick*), in which it means vomiting or ready to vomit.
In U.S. and Scotch use the wider sense is still common. . . .'
Actually this specialization appears to have begun early in the
seventeenth century, but it was the general rather than the spe-

cial meaning which was carried to America and which has prevailed there.

The word *apartment* offers another illustration of the same tendency, operating, however, with the aid of the grammatical form and functions of plurality. This term was, from 1641 on, applied to a portion of a house or building consisting of a suite of rooms allotted to the use of a particular family. *Apartment* still has this meaning in the United States. In England, beginning in 1715, *apartment* seems to have been confined in meaning to a single room, the older sense of a suite of rooms being expressed by the term *flat* or by the plural *apartments*. This plural development did not spread to the United States, where single-room quarters must be referred to as *one-room apartments*.

In those cases where America retained the older meaning of a word, the newer British meaning was not always in the direction of a greater precision, narrowness, or specialization. Quite as frequently the opposite development occurred, and the word assumed a broader significance in England. For instance, *chemist* was expanded in England to include those who prepared and sold medicinal drugs. Much the same sort of development may be observed in the word *tariff*.

Originally an Arabic word, *tariff* came into English through Italian and referred to an arithmetical table or statement, but was applied almost as early to an official list or schedule setting forth the several customs duties to be imposed on imports or exports. In England a further extension to include the list of charges at a hotel or restaurant, found as early as 1751, remains today as a common meaning of the word. Ultimately this generalization was also carried to the United States, but only to the extent that we might, in this country, conceivably speak of a hotel or railroad tariff, though we would normally do so only by employing a specifying or limiting term. *Tariff* by itself still means customs duties in the United States.

Not infrequently words acquire, in the course of time, a somewhat different status in England and America. The word *baggage* affords an excellent illustration. It came into the language early in the fifteenth century and meant what is now called 'luggage' in England. This meaning has survived as the ordinary term in the United States; it died out in England at the close of the eighteenth century. A special military use, 'the portable equipment of an army,' continues in England as well as in the United States, but in general the most striking English developments were unfavorable. Such meanings as 'rubbish,' 'purulent or corrupt matter,' 'trashy article,' all appear in sixteenth-century English use. Just a bit later it was applied to a disreputable woman, a strumpet; citations for this range from Shakespeare to Thackeray. Only a very mild and playful version of this epithet came to America—witness Irving's 'a pretty, soft-hearted baggage' —and this is pretty well obsolete. But American English has no less than twenty-five combinations for *baggage* meaning 'luggage.'

A word may begin to change its status by being typed as something other than upper-class speech. This happened to *jack* for 'knave' in cards. The ordinary term in the United States is *jack*. The word was first used in this sense in the game of *all fours,* some time in the seventeenth century. A little later it spread for a time to all card games, and apparently it was this broadened meaning that was carried to America. By 1861, however, we find Estella in *Great Expectations* saying with disdain, 'He calls the knaves, Jacks, this boy!' and currently it is classified as non-upper-class English speech.

The development of an unfavorable meaning in a word is called pejoration. There are several dramatic instances of such change in British English, occurring in words which have retained their older, relatively neutral significance in the United States. Students of the theater will recall the furor created by George Bernard Shaw when, early in the twentieth century, he had one of the characters in *Pygmalion* use the word *bloody.* No American could possibly appreciate this; the word is quite neutral here, but as Mencken has said, 'in England it is regarded as indecent, with overtones of the blasphemous.' Its history is briefly outlined by the *Oxford English Dictionary* as follows: 'In general use from the Restoration to 1750. Now constantly in the mouths of the lowest classes, but by respectable people considered a horrid word.' For a while, at least, *stomach* acquired taboo characteristics in England and was avoided in ordinary conversation. None of these pejorative developments have occurred on the American continent, where the words retain their older neutral and unblemished character.

The opposite semantic development, namely where a word in the course of time becomes less objectionable, or even positively more respectable, is called amelioration. This seems to have occurred in England with respect to the word *nasty*, which in its original sense meant 'foul, filthy, dirty.' Today it is greatly toned down, often indicating nothing more than that which is somewhat unpleasant or mildly disagreeable. American use is still generally closer to the earlier meaning.

The word *lobbyist* presents an even more striking instance of British amelioration, this time of a term which is really American in origin. It was coined to apply to those who frequent the lobbies of the national House of Representatives, the Senate, and other lesser legislative bodies in order to influence members in the exercise of their lawmaking functions. There is in the American use of the term usually a suggestion of improper, if not sinister, influence. When the word was transferred to England and applied to the House of Commons it came to refer to a journalist frequenting the lobbies there for the purpose of picking up items of political gossip. So thoroughly did the ameliorative process operate, and so respectable did the word become, that Mencken cites an instance of a commemorative tablet in St. Bride's Church, Fleet Street, designating the honored individual as a 'Lobbyist in the Palace of Westminster and London.'

Thus far we have been concerned with words retaining older meanings in America but in which a specific direction of semantic change is visible in England. In many instances, however, the English simply discontinued employing certain senses of words, senses which are still current in America. *Fall* for 'autumn' is one of these. Its use in this sense began in England in 1545.

With reference to its present status, the *Oxford English Dictionary* comments: 'In U.S. the ordinary term for autumn; in England now rare in literary use though found in some dialects.' It is difficult to find out from the dictionary evidence just when the term did die out in England, although it seems to have been some time during the second half of the nineteenth century. There may be some merit in Horwill's suggestion that it is now used in England only when the suggestion of falling leaves makes it appropriate. At all events, this is not a case of semantic change or development in either Britain or America subsequent to the period of colonization. This particular meaning just died out in British English.

The word *raise* offers another interesting instance of the same tendency. As Horwill very aptly commented, 'In England one grows farm or garden products, breeds animals, and rears children. In America one raises them all.' Curiously enough, *raise* was once used in all these senses in England. With the meaning 'breed' it is recorded up to 1767; with the meaning 'rear,' up to 1795; and with the meaning 'grow,' as late as 1875. All of these extensions of meaning seem to have been somewhat sporadic seventeenth- and eighteenth-century developments, at which time they were transported westward, and though soon dying out in England, gained strength and became a permanent fixture of the language of the Americans.

Further illustrations are afforded by the verb *clod* as applied to soils. Citations for British use range from 1530 to 1741, but this meaning is still current in America. *Quit,* in the sense of 'to stop' does not continue in England after 1754. *Cabin,* now confined to nautical use in England, meant 'a poor dwelling' only up to 1832. If nothing else, the title of Harriet Beecher Stowe's famous work has served to perpetuate it in the United States.

In the general area of pronunciation, the American variety of English is equally notable for its perpetuation of older features of the language. This is true, for example, of the two sounds which offer the most marked difference between British English, at least of the south-country variety, and the language spoken by the majority of Americans: namely, the vowels of *fast, bath, calf,* and *aunt* on the one hand, and those of *earth, turn, firm,* and *word* on the other.

The words in the first group are pronounced in what Wyld and Jones have termed Received Standard [British] English with the stressed vowel of *father,** and generally in American English with the vowel of *cat.*† It is believed by most authorities that the language of Shakespeare contained no 'broad' [ɑ] sounds whatsoever. Accordingly, the *fast, calf, bath* group of words was pronounced in England of the sixteenth century as it is in most of America today. There is some disagreement over the precise way in which and the time at which the broad [ɑ] developed, but there is reason for believing that even as late as the mid-eighteenth century it had not yet been adopted. Sheridan's pronouncing dictionary, published in 1780, gives no indication of the existence of an [ɑ] vowel in England for words of this group. The work of Batchelor, as late as 1809, is likewise lacking in such evidence. On the American side of the ocean, the vowel of *cat,* [æ], appears even for words like *father* and *hardly* in the phonetic alphabet devised in 1768 by that versatile genius, Benjamin Franklin. Twenty years later, Noah Webster in his famous spelling book still indicated the [æ] pronunciation for *aunt, jaunt,* and *sauce.*

Nevertheless, soon after 1800 the [ɑ] vowel slowly established itself in British English, at least in that variety spoken in the vicinity of London. There is some evidence pointing to the ironical circumstance that it originated in Cockney speech— ironical because in America the 'broad' pronunciation is frequently interpreted as an indication of refinement, especially by the socially and culturally insecure. Walker, for example, in his pronouncing dictionary of 1790 characterizes this pronunciation of the vowel as vulgar, and the so-called flat *a* as 'characteristic of the elegant and learned world.' At all events, despite a wide diversity of usage in London itself, the [ɑ] sound must have

* Transcribed with the symbol [ɑ] in the International Phonetic Alphabet.
† Transcribed with the symbol [æ] in the International Phonetic Alphabet.

gained a firm foothold in southeastern England by the second quarter of the nineteenth century. The question of its extension to coastal New England will be discussed later. The important thing to be noticed here is that American English has retained the older or earlier pronunciation feature, whereas British English, in what is sometimes called its Received Standard form, has undergone a more recent development.

In this connection it should be realized that the total number of words pronounced with the vowel of *cat* in American English but with that of *father* in British English is relatively small. There are possibly not more than 150 altogether that are in common use, as compared with at least three times as many which regularly have the [æ] vowel in both American and British English. *Hat, lamb, sand, bag, cap, ham,* and *hand* for instance invariably have the 'flat' or fronted vowel sound, although some few Americans make themselves ridiculous by giving these the [ɑ] sound in their misguided but valiant attempts to assume a British pronunciation. Conversely, the historical short *a* has regularly become [ɑ] before *r* and in a few other isolated words in both Britain and America. For the most part the words which vary between the flat and the broad *a* are those in which the vowel is followed by a voiceless fricative (*f, s,* or *th,* as in *thin*) or by *n.*

The same general conclusion holds for the differences between Received Standard British and general American practice in such words as *firm, earth, turn,* and *word.* Originally these had the vowel indicated by their present spelling followed by consonantal *r.* Thus, *firm* would have had the vowel of *bit, earth* the vowel of *get, turn* the vowel of *good,* and *word* the vowel of *fork.* * There is some reason for believing that by Shakespeare's time the various vowels had begun to coalesce with the following *r* to produce a vowel something like our present-day sound of *err;* † in fact, there is evidence for its existence in London lower or lower-middle class dialect as early as 1560.

* Pronounced [fɪrm], [erθ], [tʊrn], and [wɔrd] respectively.

† Transcribed [ɝ] in the International Phonetic Alphabet as adapted to American English.

This vowel is made with the jaw in approximately mid-position, with the tongue neither excessively advanced nor retarded, but with its point usually turned upward toward the roof of the mouth. It is this inverted or retroflex position of the tongue that gives the sound its *r*-like quality. Presumably, as time went on, the vowel of *err* came to be pronounced in southern England with the tongue less and less inverted, until by the close of the eighteenth century, the *r*-coloring appears to have been lost altogether.* The same development took place with *r* before consonants, as in *ford*, and after vowels in word-final position, as in *far.*†

We learn, for example, from Walker's *Rhyming Dictionary* of 1775 that *aunt* and *haunch* were pronounced 'nearly as if written *arnt* and *harnch.*' This does not mean that an *r* was inserted in *aunt* but rather that the *r* of *aren't* was scarcely audible at this time. And in his *Pronouncing Dictionary* of 1791 the same lexicographer tells us that, 'in England, and particularly in London, the *r* in *bar, bard, card, regard,* etc., is pronounced so much in the throat as to be little more than the middle or Italian *a*, lengthened into *baa, baad, caad, regaad.*' He adds that in London, 'It is sometimes entirely sunk.'

Whether these statements are interpreted to mean that at this time British English had merely a weakened *r* or had lost the sound altogether does not matter greatly. The point is that the English *r*'s were losing their retroflex quality, one which has been retained in the speech of the vast majority of Americans. Here, as with the flat *a*, American English has preserved a feature of the language which was subsequently altered in British English.

A few other less obvious differences between the stressed vowels of American and British English point to the same general conclusion. The vowel of British English *sun* and *cut* is more open than the corresponding American sound; it is made with the jaw in a slightly lower position and possibly with the tongue somewhat more advanced, giving it a timbre more like that of

* Transcribed [ɜ] in the International Phonetic Alphabet.
† Pronounced [fɔːd] or [fɔəd] and [faː] in the so-called *r*-less dialects. [ː] indicates increased duration of the sound in question.

the sound of [ɑ]. During the last 500 years this sound has developed from one which was undoubtedly like our present stressed vowel in the word *good,* made with the jaw in fairly close or high position and with the tongue concentrated or bunched in the back of the mouth. It is fairly evident, therefore, that in British English the sound has undergone the more radical modification and that American English undoubtedly preserves an intermediate stage in its development.

Likewise the marked tendency in American English, or at least in some areas of the United States, to pronounce the so-called 'short *o*' with an [ɑ]-like quality in words like *got, crop, hot, God, stock,* and *frog,* appears to have had its origin in a fashionable pronunciation of the seventeenth century. The difference between British and American pronunciation here is chiefly one of lip-rounding, the vowels being pronounced with spread lips in American English and with slightly pursed or rounded lips in England. The comedies of the Restoration period abound in spellings suggesting unrounded pronunciations of the vowels in these words, both by the fops and the true-wit characters. Moreover, there were in the seventeenth and eighteenth centuries a number of books on English pronunciation written for foreigners who wanted to learn English. In these, English short *o* is very often equated with French or German *a,* also suggesting a pronunciation with spread instead of rounded lips. Again American English seems to preserve a feature of the language characteristic of British English pronunciation 200 or 300 years ago, although in this particular instance British pronunciation could be considered as preserving an even older variety of the sound.

In the matter of unstressed syllables, the chief difference in the pronunciation of the two countries is to be found in the greater retention of secondary stress in American English. British English tends to collapse the third syllable of words like *secretary, necessary, millinery, dictionary, oratory,* and at times to reduce the secondary stress of such other plurisyllables as *circumstance* or *corroborative.* The presence of secondary stress in the *-ary, -ery, -ory* words in the pronunciation of Shakespeare is indicated by the prosody of Hamlet's famous line, 'Customary suits of solemn black.' Cooper in 1685 and Elphinston as late as 1765 still indicated the presence of secondary stress in these words. Here too the elimination of the secondary stress appears to have been a late-eighteenth- and early-nineteenth-century development in England not shared by speakers of American English.

It seems also that the pronunciation of the final syllables of words like *fertile* and *hostile* with the sound of *file* is a fairly recent British development. Earlier authorities on pronunciation generally indicate the vowel of *fill* for the second syllable of these words—the general practice in the United States today. Turning for a moment to the consonants, we may observe that the initial *wh* combination in such words as *whale* and *wharf* is quite regularly simplified to *w* in southern British English, but in the United States there is a much stronger tendency to retain the earlier pronunciation.

British-American differences in the pronunciation of individual words rather than those representing a whole class of sounds usually show the present British pronunciation to be the more recent development. This is true, for example, of *hover*, regularly pronounced in America with the vowel of *cut*, but often in England with the vowel of *hot*. The derivation of this word is uncertain, but early spellings leave little doubt that the present American pronunciation is the traditional one. Similarly, the American pronunciation of *schedule*, with *sk* rather than *sh*, appears to have been an earlier British pronunciation. The one now prevailing in England was probably generally adopted during the second quarter of the nineteenth century.

The spelling bee, a prominent factor in American colonial and frontier life, is sometimes advanced as a possible explanation of certain phonetic features of American English. It is argued that the practice of spelling and pronouncing words a syllable at a time could have been responsible for the retention of strong secondary stress as well as the maintenance of the retroflex quality in our *r* sounds. The latter is particularly questionable.

The coastal New Englander calls the letter *r*, 'ah.' Consequently, when he spells the word *farm* and indicates the third letter as 'ah,' he is not likely to put any more retroflexion into his pronunciation of the complete word. With respect to the unstressed syllables, it must be remembered that the few groups of words wherein British and American English differ in the assignment of stress constitute only a small minority of the English plurisyllables. If spelling *complete* and *explanation* a syllable at a time did not result in establishing the vowel of *hot* for *com-* in the first, and the vowel of *pan* for *-plan-* in the second, there is no real reason for assuming that our vigorous *-ary* in *dictionary* can be satisfactorily explained in this manner.

The preponderance of immigrant stocks learning English in the new world has also been advanced as an explanation of these American tendencies. It has been assumed that first and second generation speakers of English were more likely to pronounce words just as they were spelled. But again, one can see no compelling reason for the retention of the particular features of older English which are present in American pronunciation when any one of a dozen other notorious deviations from spelling might have been adopted as well.

In certain of its structural aspects, also, American English appears to reflect earlier stages of the language. There are, it is true, relatively few inflectional differences in the standard forms of British and American, but one of the most prominent will illustrate the general principle to which this chapter is devoted. British English has but one past participle for the verb *get*, namely the form *got*. American English has, in addition, the form *gotten*, which no speaker of British English ever uses in the first place, and which many Britons assume, moreover, to be the only American form. Consequently English novelists frequently portray American characters using *gotten* in situations where the word would never occur in normal American speech.

In fact, most Americans regularly make a very precise distinction between *got* and *gotten*. 'We've *got* ten thousand dollars for laboratory equipment,' means that the funds in question are in

our possession—we have them. 'We have *gotten* ten thousand
dollars for laboratory equipment,' means that we have obtained
or acquired this particular sum of money. Few Americans would
have the slightest question about the difference in the meaning
of these two sentences.

Get is a so-called strong verb which, in the process of normal
development, would normally have had a form like *gat* for the
past tense (which is actually the case in the Authorized Version
of the Bible) and *geten* or *getten* as its past participle. Somehow
or other the verb was reworked or re-formed according to the
pattern of such verbs as *bear* and *tear;* it developed *got* as its
past-tense form and *got* or *gotten* as its past participle. In England *gotten* seems not to have continued in use beyond the mid
or late seventeenth century, but Americans have continued to
employ it up to the present time. So much for the purely formal
aspect of the construction; there is a syntactical element to be
considered as well.

After the verb *have* came to be more widely used as an
auxiliary, it tended to lose force as an indicator of possession.
Consequently the verb *get* in its perfect tense form tended, during the sixteenth century, to shift its meaning from acquisition
to that of possession, much as Spanish *tener* replaced *haber*. The
Oxford English Dictionary cites Shakespeare, Swift, Dr. Johnson,
Thackeray, and Ruskin to illustrate the possessive use of *have
got*. This seems to have spread to America soon after its development, although even today some Americans mistakenly feel that
the construction is somewhat less elegant or less correct than the
simple verb *have*, and virtually no American naturally uses *had
got* as the equivalent of *had*. 'He had not got a shilling for the
meter,' becomes 'He didn't have . . .' in American English.
Moreover, the continued existence of the older *gotten* made possible the distinction between *have got* and *have gotten* in America, which the English, confined to the single form *got*, could not
develop in precisely the same manner.

Another structural difference between American and British
English is to be found in the much stronger tendency in the

latter toward the use of plural verbs and plural pronouns of reference with collective nouns. Words like *government, ministry, cabinet, company, corporation,* and names of athletic teams regularly govern the plural rather than the singular number. A sentence such as, 'The government *are* acting like *themselves,*' quoted from Southey by the *Oxford English Dictionary,* is characteristically British and quite impossible for an American who, if he is surprised by the foregoing, will be downright startled by the sporting headline, 'JESUS ROW TO EASY VICTORY.'

No one seems to have studied the development of the plural with these collectives. Originally the singular would have been demanded, but as early as 1000, plural verbs began to appear with collective nouns when the idea of a number of individuals took precedence over the group concept. This is the way collectives were used in Shakespeare's time, and it is the way they are still used in the United States. The consistent use of the plural with certain of these nouns apparently developed in England in the second quarter of the nineteenth century. Southey is the *Oxford English Dictionary* source for plural agreement with *corporation* as well as *government. Ministry* appears in this construction somewhat later. American English has retained the older practice, and as yet no indications of a change have appeared.

The tendency of American English to retain older features of the language needs no further elaboration. We have found evidence of it in the vocabulary, in pronunciation, in inflectional forms, and in syntax. Nor is English the only language in which a colonial offshoot shows a tendency toward archaism. Canadian French reflects features of continental French antedating the revolution. Older elements of European Spanish may be seen in the current idiom of any number of Latin American countries, and it is well known that modern Icelandic has been less affected by linguistic change than Norwegian of the present day.

Moreover, if we turn from language to certain other aspects of our natural life, we find that America has kept alive a number of elements of its cultural heritage which are quite absent, or at best much less conspicuous, in the England of today than at the time they were brought to this country.

The religious or theological background of the colonies provides an excellent case in point. During the early settlement of New England, the Calvinism of Cromwell and his followers was the dominating force in the mother country. It has been characterized by Max Savelle as, 'the major item in the religious inheritance of the Americans from Great Britain.' The Puritanism of New England was later reinforced by the Calvinism of the Dutch and the Scotch-Irish, both of whom came in considerable numbers and were influential in our subsequent development. 'Today,' says Russell Blankenship, 'Puritanism as a religious faith has quite largely disappeared from New England as it has from other parts of the country, but it exists all over the nation as a moral force, an influence constantly directing our attention to the fact that life is a most serious business and that everything must be judged in terms of current morality. In this respect Puritanism is still a strong force in American life and thought.'

The blood feud, which provides the motivation for many of the ballads, chronicles, and other literature of Scotland and the border counties, appears in a sense to have been reactivated in the Kentucky and West Virginia mountains about the third quarter of the last century. The violent hatreds and gory exploits of the Hatfields and the McCoys have virtually become folk legend in the United States, and certain aspects of the saga (such as its origin in a quarrel over the ownership of a pig) have a quaintly humorous flavor. This particular altercation was merely the most notorious of a fairly large number. Both the racial stock of the participants and the settlement history of the entire mountain area leave little question that Kentucky feuding was in essence a transference and prolongation of the same culture trait from the Scottish border country.

A less dramatic but even more characteristic transference is found in American patchwork quilt patterns, many of which preserve figures and designs which were brought over from England. Miss Elizabeth King, in her pamphlet *Quilting*, comments:

The 'feather' quilting pattern, it is said, is one that the women
of Northumberland have used since 1600. This is rather interesting, for the feather is one that is found on many early American quilts, and is still one of the most popular designs used
today. So that we can well assume that some colonist from
Northumberland brought it with her when she came to the
new world.

Without question other patterns would, upon investigation,
reveal a similar history. At all events, quilt making is still practiced in many parts of the United States. Homemade quilts are
regularly exhibited at our county fairs. On the other hand, in
preparing for a British exposition held not so very long ago,
officials experienced some difficulty in finding throughout England proper, much evidence that the craft was still being carried
on. Again we have kept alive a culture trait which for a time,
at least, was disappearing in the mother country.

A final and well-known illustration of the preservation of old-
country ways in America is offered by the folk ballads. According
to Cyclone Covey, who wrote the chapter on music in Max
Savelle's excellent cultural history, *Seeds of Liberty*:

> Folk-traditions are so conservative that many tens of thou-
> sands of people throughout America today sing and play (along-
> side later songs and tunes) folk music of their ancestors of the
> seventeenth and eighteenth centuries. They sing about char-
> acters and settings of fairytale remoteness—knights and ghosts;
> Robin Hood, Prince Charlie, and Henry V; Londontown and
> the banks of Dundee . . . In the great majority of cases folk-
> songs were kept alive by the women, who sang them as they
> worked or to entertain or to lull to sleep their children. The
> exacting conservatism of children has been an important factor
> in the relative changelessness of the songs over so extended
> a period.°

According to Covey at least fifty-five separate airs have been
transported and preserved, the well-known *Barbara Allen* existing in the largest numbers of both tunes and texts.

° Pp. 539–40.

These post-colonial survivals of earlier phases of mother-country culture, taken in conjunction with the retention of earlier linguistic features, have made what I should like to call a colonial lag. I mean to suggest by this term nothing more than that in a transplanted civilization, as ours undeniably is, certain features which it originally possessed remain static over a period of time. Transplanting usually results in a time lag before the organism, be it a geranium or a brook trout, becomes adapted to its new environment. There is no reason why the same principle should not apply to a people, their language, and their culture.

To say that a lag operated, in language as well as in other cultural facets of our national life, does not necessarily imply agreement with Ortega y Gasset, who once described American civilization as purely colonial and as derivate as a hollow ball. In fact, it is not even necessary to agree with John Fiske that there is a lag in the total development of American culture. As we shall see in the chapter which follows, Krapp was quite right in turning from Fiske to Turner—that is, from the preservation of the archaic to the inventiveness of the frontier—as the guiding philosophy of his treatment of the English language in America. Nevertheless, in order to maintain a properly balanced point of view, the existence of the colonial lag cannot be ignored.

5

Yankee Ingenuity and the Frontier Spirit

The influence of the frontier has been considered so important an element in our national life that a whole school of historians, following the lead of Frederick Jackson Turner, has come to interpret our national development in terms of the so-called frontier thesis. Turner himself has stated his position as follows:

> Thus the advance of the frontier has meant a steady influence away from the influence of Europe, a steady growth of independence on American lines. And to study this advance, the men who grew up under these conditions, and the political, economic, and social results of it, is to study the really American part of our history.

So too in the historical study of American literature, there has been a tendency to interpret as products of the frontier those writers who were most inclined to strike out in original directions and whose works reflect the greatest independence of conventional Continental literary tradition. In all this we must remember that somewhere or other, facing the English-speaking settlers in the new world, there was a frontier for a period of nearly three centuries, from the beginning of the seventeenth until almost the close of the nineteenth.

Similarly, foreign borrowings and the maintenance of older

words, meanings, and pronunciations, representing the incorpora-
tion of non-English elements and the retention of older phases
of the culture of our mother country, fail to explain much of
what is most characteristic of the English language in America.
The language historian must also concern himself particularly
with the innovations in the English language which have developed on this side of the Atlantic. These are evident chiefly
in the vocabulary, but it will be found that matters of grammar
and structure enter into the problem as well.

A development in the field of grammar can serve as the first
illustration. This is the phenomenon that is sometimes called
functional change. In most languages various parts of speech
have what might be termed characteristic shapes. Thus, in Spanish so many nouns end in *-o* and *-a* that these endings come to
be felt as definite marks of the substantive. Verb infinitives
generally end in *-ar, -er,* and *-ir,* and these terminations in their
turn are associated with the verbal function. It is possible for a
Spanish noun to become transformed into a verb, or even for the
reverse process to take place, but the transition does involve
an alteration of what has been called the characteristic shape
of the word, and consequently such changes are not too common.

English, on the other hand, has lost its inflections to such a
degree that transitions from noun to adjective, from verb to
noun, from adjective to verb, and in fact, in almost all conceiv-
able directions, are made constantly. They are so thoroughly an
ingrained part of the language that a word such as *down* may
actually perform five different part-of-speech functions: preposition, adverb, adjective, noun, and verb.

Occasionally such a transformation falls into disfavor. This has
happened to *contact* used as a verb, which is frowned upon as
commercial or possibly journalistic jargon by many people today.
However, where one word will acquire a temporary taboo, a
dozen others will shift their functions without attracting unfavorable notice. In a good many instances functional changes of this
nature have occurred in American English but not in British, or

some time has elapsed before the word appeared in its changed function in England.

Undoubtedly the most frequent type of change which is encountered is that of noun to adjective, or perhaps it would be more accurate to say the use of nouns in an adjunct or joined function. For example, almost as soon as the noun *caucus* had become a part of the American English vocabulary, it was employed in the combinations *caucus men* (1762) and *caucus clubs* (1763). This tendency is evidenced particularly in headlines, where such astounding combinations as CLUB FIGHT BLOCKS RIVER RAIL TUBE PLAN (organizational dispute interferes with plans for a rail tunnel under the river) greet the eye from time to time. A verbatim citation taken from the luncheon menu of a metropolitan department store, *Butter Cream Frosted Devil's Food Pecan Layer Cake*, illustrates an extension of the same tendency to some of our food terms. This same type of conversion occurs in British as well as American English, according to some observers, though not necessarily involving the same words, and instances of the tendency as extreme as those just given are undoubtedly less frequent.

The shift in the opposite direction, from adjective to noun, is neatly illustrated by the following advertisement from a current newspaper, which is headed BASIC DRESSES, and then goes on to read, 'A group of conservatively styled basics to accessorize as you will.' An earlier illustration of the same type of change is offered by *personal*, referring to a newspaper item, cited in 1864.

The conversion of nouns to verbs is also very common. *Clapboard* is recorded as a verb as early as 1637, which must have been not long after the colonists began to cut and plane timber into finished building materials. The verbal use of *scalp* occurred early; *tomahawk*, also reflecting Indian methods of warfare, appears as a verb in 1711. Other aspects of colonial and frontier life are reflected by *portage*, 1836, *lynch*, 1835, *deed*, 1806. The reluctance toward changes of this nature is well illustrated in connection with the last word. It was included in John Pickering's *Vocabulary or Collection of Words and Phrases Which*

Have Been Supposed to be Peculiar to the United States of America, which, appearing in 1816, was one of the earliest lists of Americanisms. Pickering's comment with reference to *deed* is, 'We sometimes hear this word used colloquially; but rarely. except by illiterate people.'

On occasion the conversion of noun into verb had to await the development of a special American meaning. This was true with *lumber.* In England the noun *lumber* meant cumbrous, useless material, apparently having been formed from the verb *to lumber.* In America, however, very early in the colonial period, the noun *lumber* was applied to cut timber. Finally, in the nineteenth century, *to lumber* came to be used both transitively and intransitively, meaning to be in the lumber business or to cut the timber off a piece of land. Likewise, *to stag it*—that is, for a man to attend a mixed party alone—could only have developed from the noun *stag,* 'a man not escorting a lady,' which in turn grew out of such combinations as *stag dance, stag dinner, stag party*— all peculiar to America. *Interview* as a verb is an American development of the special journalistic use of the noun; both are first cited in 1869. For at least the first two decades of their existence both verb and noun were quite regularly enclosed in quotation marks, and in England were used only in a somewhat jocular sense.

Nor has the process diminished with the years. Though not exclusively American, the noun *thumbtack* is commonly used in the United States for what is more frequently called a *drawing pin* in England, but the verb *to thumbtack* has thus far been cited only from American sources, from 1931 on. Likewise in this country *automobile* as a verb (1898) followed hard upon the heels of the application of the term to the self-propelled vehicle in 1895.

The frequency of this type of change may be explained in part by the fact that most of the accretions to the American vocabulary from other languages were nouns; so too are many of the compound and derivative formations. Once a thing is named, we are likely to require as well a term for its operative or verbal aspect, and functional change provides an easy solution to the problem.

The development of nouns from verbs is somewhat less common, although instances are by no means lacking. The noun *dump* as a place for waste and refuse was formed from the verb as early as 1784. The verb *sashay*, borrowed from French in 1836, was converted into a noun in 1900. As we have seen, Thoreau is credited with the first American citation of the English dialect verb *drool* in 1854; the earliest citation for *drool* as a substantive is 1867. The verb *scoop* in its journalistic sense developed as a specialization of the slang meaning, 'to get the advantage of,' which later gave rise to the noun *scoop* for a so-called newspaper 'beat,' and in fact this use of the noun *beat* came about in precisely the same way. Similarly, *release* as a noun indicating a news story given out for publication is first recorded in 1907, only three years after the earliest citation of the verb in this special journalistic sense. *Strike* used as a noun, both in baseball and in American bowling, has clearly developed from the verb; so has *cut*, meaning a reduction in prices or wages.

Drive used substantively in connection with cattle, logs, an organized campaign for collecting funds, or in the more general senses of initiative or an impulse, is a striking illustration of the development of a noun from a verb in the United States. *Probe*, meaning an investigation, appears to have been as great a favorite with headline writers at the beginning of the century as it is today. *Pick-up* for a light delivery truck is a recent (1944) instance of the same tendency.

Other types of functional change include developments of verb to adjective as in *hurry call, hurry consignment*, or even *hurry-up wagon*, a slang term for a police car; and from adjective to verb, illustrated by *to prep*, from *prep*, adjective, the clipped form of *preparatory school*.

In addition to its frequent alteration of word function, American English often has a peculiar manner of putting words or word elements together. Basically, of course, all the Teutonic languages are much given to compounding, although the tendency is possibly most noticeable in German because of its characteristic fashion of writing compounds as single words. Often the English equivalent for a German term happens not to be parallel in formation, as in *Feldmesskunst,* 'the science of surveying.' Even if the terms correspond exactly in the two languages, as in *Fire Insurance Company* compared with *Feuerversicherungsgesellschaft,* the German word by virtue of its length and solidity impresses one with its compound construction, whereas the corresponding fact in English may totally escape the writer or speaker.

Still, we do a great deal of compounding in English; it is a heritage of the oldest period in the language, when such felicitous constructions as *whale road* for 'ocean,' *hammer leaving* for 'sword,' and *peace weaver,* for 'queen,' known as kennings, constituted one of the characteristic rhetorical devices of our earliest poetry. But the device survived the purely Teutonic period of our language. A page of Shakespeare yields 'something-settled,' 'periwig-pated,' 'queen mother,' 'town crier,' and 'to out-Herod.' It has been pointed out, moreover, that although English many centuries ago replaced its original compound *book house* with the French borrowing *library,* the language has subsequently coined such combinations as *bookshop, bookbinder, bookcase, book collector, book fair, booklover, book review, bookroom, book sale,* and *book trade.* These are only a few of the 115 combinations recorded by the *Oxford English Dictionary,* to which may be added *book agent, book bindery, book count, book factor, book farmer, book farming, book concern, book peddler,* and *book social,* all of which are American in origin.

American English in particular has demonstrated a fondness for compound formations, one which not only goes back to its earliest beginnings, but which frequently seems to have the earmarks of an indigenous style. The extent to which compounding has gone on in this country is illustrated by E. H. Criswell's study of the vocabularies of the members of the Lewis and Clark expedition. This memorable journey to the then unknown Far West had a scientific as well as a political aim. All of its members were strictly enjoined to keep accurate accounts of their observations and daily proceedings. 'The problem of naming a vast number of plants, animals, topographic features, and the multiplicity of objects and institutions connected with Indian life was a real one,' comments Professor Criswell. 'They met this problem in various ingenious and interesting ways . . . They were truly linguistic pioneers, as well as pioneers in the literal and material sense.'

The importance of compounding in the linguistic operations of the Lewis and Clark company is shown by the fact that of 171 previously unrecorded Americanisms consisting of general terms, 106 are full-word combinations. Of 412 previously unrecorded American names for plants and animals, 129 are compounds. Of the 301 terms for which these journals supply earlier examples than have been previously recorded, 132 are compound words. Just a few of the combined forms culled from these journals include *arrowwood, bull snake, ground squirrel, tumble bug, cut-off, copperhead, cottonwood, catbird, bottom land, tow-cord.*

The same strong tendency toward the formation of compounds is evident from a study of the individual word-entries in the *Dictionary of Americanisms.* There are twenty compound words with *stage* as a first element, forty-seven formed from *beaver,* and over a hundred with *yellow* or with a combination already formed from the word (*yellow-dog contract*).

The whole question of compounding in American English can best be discussed in terms of the particular sectors of the vocabulary in which the process has taken place. Moreover, the creation of compounds upon a large scale in these areas seems to have been in response to several distinct classes of situations.

First of all, there were those fields in which physical conditions prevailing in America presented a considerable degree of change from those characteristic of England. For example, many of the flora and fauna in the northern part of the colonies were similar to but not identical with the plant and animal life of England. Where differences did exist, new terminology had to be provided, to which the 129 compounds of the Lewis and Clark accounts bear impressive testimony. Many of our compounds in these fields are very early: *live oak* is found in *A True Declaration of the Estate of the Colonie in Virginia,* 1610. *Bull frog* is first recorded in 1698, *ground hog* in 1656, *swamp oak* in 1681, *coach-whip snake* in 1736. Differences in topography are reflected by *bottom land,* 1728, *water gap,* 1756, *underbrush,* 1775. Even the weather is represented by *cold snap,* 1776.

Institutions also were liable to change in a new environment, and the changes brought a new terminology with them. Farming, carried on under totally different conditions, both physical and economic, developed such combinations as *log house, log cabin, corn belt, cotton gin, round up, land office, hog ranch, stump fence, worm fence, hired man, hired girl, hired hand,* and *hired help.* American independence brought in its wake the development of institutions and practices peculiar to this country. So extensive was the political and governmental terminology which resulted that a whole volume has been devoted to it: witness *lame duck, boss rule, favorite son, dark horse, carpetbagger,* and *peanut politics* as a random sampling of our new formations here.

When we consider peculiarly American developments, the proportion of compounds in the terminology becomes even greater. Baseball, in its present form a distinctively American game, applies compound terms to every specific position on the team except for the catcher and pitcher. The four bases, the home plate, the infield, the outfield, chest protectors, and various types of gloves are all compounds. There have developed, more-over, any number of compound terms associated with the game: *pinch-hit, bush league, double-header, grandstand play, college try, charley horse,* and *rain check.* Basketball, a fairly recent American invention, is just as full of compounds, as is the some-what more sedentary poker, with its *full house, straight flush, jack pot, penny ante,* and *seven-card stud.*

The first *soda fountain* seems to have originated in Boston in 1824. Ever since that time the array of ice-cream sodas, the sundaes, the banana splits, the varieties of milk shakes, malted and otherwise, has resulted in a terminology consisting almost entirely of compounds. Even *Coca-Cola,* that insidious fifth-column of American culture, originally described (1887) as a 'brain tonic and intellectual soda-fountain beverage,' has the appearance of a compound. Our cocktails and the innumerable varieties of sandwiches are equally devoted to the combined form.

A third type of situation arose when a new invention or development struck America and England at the same time, resulting in the creation of terminologies quite independent of each other. The railroad offers an early instance of this; the automobile, radio, and now television are later examples. For example, in American railroad terms there are such combinations as *boxcar, handcar, chair car, jerkwater, waybill, stopover, sideswipe, milk train, hog engine, sidetrack,* and *roundhouse.*

In conclusion we must ask whether any special qualities are discernible in the American compounds. Certainly one receives, from a listing of any number of them, the impression of a somewhat peculiar flavor. Even such a small group as *sweatshop, disk jockey, speakeasy, rat race, soap opera, zoot suit,* and *wetback* seems to have something indigenous about it when compared with British *goods van, wood wool, drop-head coupé, motor car hire service,* and *screw spanner.*

Frequently the American compound is elliptical rather than self-explanatory. *Soap opera* is not immediately clear to the uninitiated. One needs to know that romances of the boy-meets-girl type or accounts of supposedly typical American family life, presented in seemingly never-ending installments over the American air waves, are frequently sponsored by manufacturers of toilet and laundry soaps and are meant for the ear of the housewife as she goes about her daily tasks with her radio turned on. For a comprehension of *wetback,* it must be realized that annually large numbers of Mexican laborers enter the United States by the simple expedient of swimming or wading across the Rio Grande, thereby avoiding quota restrictions and immigration formalities in general. *Car hop, straw hat theater,* and *strip tease* likewise require a footnote for the foreigner.

Metaphor plays a considerable part in these American combinations. A *disk jockey* has nothing to do with horses; he is an employee of a radio station and conducts a program of recorded music. *Rat race, captive mine, ghost town, double talk* all employ one of their elements figuratively. Finally there is often a strong element of incongruity in the two or more parts comprising the combination: note *taxi-dancer, prowl car, squawk box, prairie schooner,* and *cow college.*

New words may also be formed, not by combining full or independent words but by the addition of prefixes or suffixes to a single word. Here, too, American English has found a fertile field for its inventiveness. Allen Walker Read once remarked that a history of American opposition movements could be written from the treatment of the prefix *anti-* in the *Dictionary of American English.* The newer *Dictionary of Americanisms* lists no less than 105 of these combinations, ranging all the way from *anti-federalist,* through *anti-secession* and *anti-Mormon,* up to *anti-braintruster* and *anti-C.I.O.* Other prefixes which have been particularly fruitful are *de-, pro-, semi-,* and *super-,* the last of these bearing witness to the national tendency toward hyperbole.

Some of the suffixes which have been employed to a considerable extent in American English include *-ette,* which serves the functions of a feminine marker in *farmerette, usherette, copette* (policewoman), and *drum-majorette,* and that of a dimunitive in *kitchenette, dinette,* and *bathinette.* The suffix *-ee,* usually indicating a verbal object, appears as early as 1870 in *contestee,* this time with subjective force, as also later in *escapee.* Actually, one might almost trace an American soldier's progress through World War II in terms of this suffix beginning with *draftee* or *selectee,* proceeding to *rejectee, inductee,* and *trainee,* going on to the seat of the conflict with *liberee* and *evacuee,* concluding his career as a *separatee,* and his opinion of it all as a *pollee.*

Place designation is indicated by *-ite* in *Camdenite, New Jerseyite;* but the suffix has a broader classificatory function in *socialite, laborite, trailerite,* and the punning *third-termite,* coined during the presidential election of 1940.

Both *-ster* and *-eer* seem to have acquired unfavorable connotations in *gangster, speedster* (though not in *dopester*), *racketeer, sloganeer, black and gray marketeer,* and also *blacketeer.* The suffix *-itis* is playfully pejorative in *golfitis, conventionitis, radioitis,* and *headlinitis,* but it is worth noting that *appendicitis* is also of American origin. The desire to give a professional aura to occupations deserving of somewhat less has led to formations in *-ist, -ician,* and *-tor: receptionist, cosmetist, cosmetician, beautician, mortician,* and *realtor.*

Most of the combinations mentioned so far have been nouns. The suffix *-ize* has been frequently employed to create new verbs: *itemize, accessorize, demoralize, burglarize, slenderize, simonize, winterize, hospitalize,* as well as *Americanize, Morganize, Fletcherize, Sanforize,* and *Trubenize,* based upon proper names. In this connection it is interesting to observe that as early as 1591, in his introduction to Sir Philip Sidney's *Astrophel and Stella,* Thomas Nashe castigated the 'reprehenders that complain of my boysterous compound words and ending my Italianate coined words all in *ize.*' This suggests that, in addition to the freedom from linguistic restraint naturally incident to a frontier culture, there was a like impetus stemming from the exuberance of Elizabethan English.

The suffix *-er* is undoubtedly one of the earliest to have been used to form peculiarly American coinages. A citation for 1654–5 indicates that a *corder* was a town official whose function it was to pile salable wood into standard cords. There is also an oft-repeated story about the origin of the word *schooner.* The first vessel of this type was supposedly launched about 1713 at Gloucester, Massachusetts. A bystander is said to have exclaimed, 'Oh, how she scoons!' To which the captain replied, 'A scooner let her be.'

One interesting difference between British and American English is to be found in the use of the *-ery* suffix, which in England is often used for a class of materials (*drapery*) or the place where an occupation or operation is carried on (*colliery*) but seldom for the establishment where the product is sold at retail.

Thus, *bakery* in England refers to the craft of the baker or the place for making bread, rather than to the place where baked goods are available to the consumer, as has been true of the United States since 1827. Likewise, *grocery*, used in England for the merchandise itself since the fifteenth century, was applied to a retail establishment in America as early as 1659. *Groggery* was coined in this country in 1827.

Conversely, American English uses *cook* in combinations such as *cookbook, cook stove*, where British English has *cookery*; and such familiar English terms as *ironmongery, deanery, farmery,* and *rockery* sound strange to an American ear. Moreover, some of the *-ery* combinations which do not indicate a retail establishment, though originally formed in this country, have had a short life here. *Printery* was used as early as 1638 in Massachusetts, but has now been replaced by *print shop* or when it applies to an official bureau by *printing office*. *Loggery* for a log cabin, first used in Michigan in 1839, lasted less than half a century.

Another process or device common in English is that of shortening words by clipping—the omission of syllables from the beginning or end. This had gone to such lengths in the seventeenth and early eighteenth centuries that Addison objected to it in a frequently quoted statement from one of the *Spectator* papers:

> It is perhaps this humour of speaking no more than we needs must, which has so miserably curtailed some of our words, that in familiar writings and conversations they often lose all but their first syllables, as in *mob, rep, pos, incog,* and the like; and as all ridiculous words made their first entry into a language by familiar phrases, I dare not answer for these that they will not in time be looked upon as a part of our tongue.

Despite this protest, which was echoed if not anticipated by Swift in one of the *Tatler* essays and in his *Proposal for Correcting the English Tongue,* and repeated as much as a half-century later by the rhetorician Campbell, the tendency has continued on both sides of the Atlantic. The English have contributed *cab, photo, spats, van,* and *wig* to the language, to mention only a few. The erroneous notion that this shortening process was indigenous to the United States was set forth at the turn of the century by the Boston *Herald*, which declared in its issue of July 4, 1899, 'If we must Americanise and shorten the word, why not call them "autos?"' The point is that the Americans and the British have not always clipped the same words.

Nevertheless the mistaken notion of the Boston newspaper is understandable, for in noting the dates of the earliest appearances of some of our commonest words in this category, one comes to realize how common the practice was just at that time. *Co-ed* put in its first appearance in 1889, *fan* for 'an enthusiast' in 1896, *gym* in 1897, *after* for 'afternoon' in 1902, *gyp* for 'gypsum water' in 1904, *gas* for 'gasoline' in 1905, and *movie* in 1906. This last item suggests also the short-lived *talkie*, first appearing in 1913. A recent clipping is that of *prefab*, 1942. These are all shortenings which have retained the initial part of the word and have eliminated the final portion.

The reverse process is seen in *sang* for 'ginseng', 1843, *stogie* for 'Conestoga' (boot or cigar), 1847, *pike* for 'turnpike' in 1852—the application of this to the road itself rather than to the bar or the toll is peculiarly American—*phone* in 1886, *coon* for 'raccoon,' *possum* for 'opossum,' and *pop* for 'soda-pop.' The word *muskellunge* has the rare distinction of appearing with either end clipped: *lunge* is found as early as 1851 in a Vermont statute; *musky* in 1894. The process goes on continuously, but the rate at which the words are adopted into the standard language varies a great deal.

A special analogical type of the shortening process has come to be known as back formation. It operates as follows: there are in English a large number of verbs ending in -*ate* which have corresponding derivative noun forms in -*ation*. Thus we have *create, creation; deviate, deviation; bifurcate, bifurcation; placate, placation; ruminate, rumination*. This gives rise to a pattern of verb in -*ate* alongside of the noun in -*ation*. The English language has, however, borrowed a few nouns in -*ation* for which the corresponding verb in -*ate* did not originally exist. When, from a noun of this type, the corresponding verb in *-ate* is then created, this process is called back formation.

It was in this fashion that the verb *donate* was formed from the noun *donation*. It first appeared in America in 1795, almost a century before any British writer ventured to use it. As late as 1935 Herbert Horwill called it 'a word which in England is eschewed by good writers as a pretentious and magniloquent vulgarism. In America on the other hand, it has acquired a place in the vocabulary of quite respectable terms.' Earlier, however, it had the dubious distinction of a place in William Cullen Bryant's famous *Index Expurgatorius* and was denounced by Richard Grant White. Today it is firmly established in the United States.

Undoubtedly the earliest of all known American back formations is *locate*, which appeared in a Virginia travel account in 1652. The noun *location* had been taken over into English more than a half-century earlier. Among the early users of *locate* were Benjamin Franklin and George Washington; it acquired respectability in a shorter time and with less of a struggle than some later formations of precisely the same character. *Commute* in the sense of regular railroad travel from a suburban residence into the city developed in a similar manner from *commutation* (ticket, train, etc.) in 1865.

Verbal nouns with other variations of the final *-tion* suffix have given us *locomote*, once slang but now obsolete, *electrocute* in 1889, *emote*, labeled jocose by Webster in 1934, and *injunct*, excoriated by Schele de Vere (a collector of Americanisms) in 1871 as 'a violent contraction.' He was equally displeased with *excurt* from *excursion*, though he failed to mention *excur*, formed twenty years earlier from the same noun.

From agentive nouns ending in *-er*, we have acquired *to housekeep*, 1842, and *to burgle*, 1870, almost a decade before *The Pirates of Penzance* where Gilbert immortalized the word in the chorus of the policemen, 'When the enterprising burglar's not a-burgling.' *To baby-sit*, possibly the most recent member of this category (except for *to student-teach*) was brought to life by the shortage of domestic help in the United States, forcing mothers to depend upon *baby sitters* to care for their children.

Miscellaneous creations include *enthuse*, probably coined in this country by a Scotsman in 1827, *jell*, 1869, and *reune*, 'to attend a reunion,' cited as colloquial in 1929. In general, back formations are not numerous; they are confined mainly to two or three types of suffixes. Some arouse violent objections and remain on the periphery of respectability for a considerable period. Others die out after a short time, but on the whole back formations have contributed their measure of utility to the American variety of English.

American ingenuity has found a much more fertile field in the telescoping of words, to produce what are sometimes known as blends. As with the other changes in form which have been discussed in this chapter, the process is employed in England as well, but not with the same words or word elements. Lewis Carroll amused himself with such coinages as *chortle*, combining *chuckle* with *snort*, and *snark* with its suggestion of *snake* and *shark*. To them he applied the label 'portmanteau words,' which he explained as follows in *Through the Looking Glass*: 'Well, "slithy" means "lithe" and "slimy" . . . You see it's like a portmanteau . . . there are two meanings packed up into one word.' And a little later in the same work: ' "Mimsy" is "flimsy" and "miserable" (there's another portmanteau for you).'

Several types of word blending may be recognized. First, there are words which combine a single syllable or two syllables of an initial word with a full or complete second term. Among these are such recent coinages as *giropilot, moto-rustler,* and *stratochamber. Amerindian* is first cited in 1897.

Possibly somewhat more common are combinations of a complete initial word with part of a second. One of the earliest instances of these recalls an interesting bit of American political history. *Gerrymander* was coined in 1812 from the name of the then governor of Massachusetts, Elbridge Gerry, and the word *salamander.* This was in reference to the peculiarly shaped election district in the northeastern part of the state, devised to maintain a majority for the political party then in control.

Other instances of this same process include *cablegram* (cable telegram) 1868, *travelogue* (travel monologue) 1903, *newscast* (news broadcast) 1937, *Airacuda* (a fighter bomber named for the barracuda) 1937, *pianothon* 1939, *camporee* (camp jamboree) 1940, *hydramatic, longram, campership, paratrooper, airathon, inspectoscope,* and *Skycycle.*

The initial portion of a first word may be combined with the final part of a second, as in *urinalysis,* 1889, *citrange* (citron, orange) 1904, *motel* (motor hotel), *celtuce* (celery, lettuce). Clare Luce's coinage *globaloney* (global baloney), *trainasium* (training gymnasium), *racon* (radar beacon), *tiglon* (tiger, lion), and *elevon* (elevator, aileron) are further examples of the same combination pattern. For combinations of this type and those which follow in the discussion, the term *acronym* has recently been coined. Also included among the acronyms are combinations of the initial syllables of two or more words. *Minicam* (miniature camera), *amtrac* (amphibious tractor), *shoran* (short range radar), and *loran* (long range navigation) are instances of this kind of blend.

In place of syllables, initial letters frequently furnish the basis for acronyms, and the words so formed may be treated in a number of ways. They may be pronounced as a word, as in *radar* (radio detection and ranging), *UNESCO, CARE* (Co-operative for American Remittances to Europe), *asdic* (anti-submarine detection investigation committee), *voder* (voice operation demonstrator), *Socony* (Standard Oil Company of New York), *USAFI, USIS,* and *NATO.* If the word so formed does not lend itself easily to pronunciation, as will frequently happen when consonants are grouped together, the letters themselves may be pronounced, as in *DP* (displaced person), *DDT* (dichloro-diphenyl-trichlorocthane), and more recently, *ACTH.* Such a combination may be concealed by spelling out the pronunciation usually given to the letters involved, as was done with the *Sea-*

bees (C.B., construction battalion) and the *Elsies* (L.C., landing craft) of World War II, or as the Standard Oil Company does with its various *Esso* (S.O.) products. A combination of the two processes just described is to be found in *Veep* (V.P.) for vice-president and *Deke* for Delta Kappa Epsilon.

Repetition of letters may be indicated by numbers: *Tri-Delt, Triple A, Four C's* (Conference on College Composition and Communication). At times vowels may be arbitrarily inserted in a series of unpronounceable consonants, as in *Huff-Duff*, the pronunciation given by servicemen to the initials *HF DF* (high frequency direction finder).

Blending has been a favorite outlet for the ingenuity of manufacturers and distributors in coining unique terms for their products. *Socony* and the *Esso* products have already been mentioned. Rival companies vie with *Mobilgas, Mobiloil, Sunoco, Enarco* (National Refining Company). Other types of merchandise give us *Nabisco, Duco, Delco, Spam, Calavo, Sealpackerchief, Band-aid, Alka-seltzer, Webcor, Philco, Aluvac, Starlac*. Any single issue of an American newspaper or magazine will supply dozens of examples.

Scientific terms are often so long and cumbersome that abbreviation of some kind must be resorted to, particularly when they are used by the lay public in non-technical situations or when they are made commercially available. Thus *ACE* becomes a convenient short reference for *a*drenal *c*ortex *e*xtract, *DOCA* for *d*esoxycorticosterone *a*cetate, *OMPA* for *o*ctomethyl *p*yrophos-*a*ramide, *ACTH* for *a*drenocorticotropic *h*ormone, and certainly one can appreciate the desirability of creating the blend word *cortisone* if he realizes that it is 17-hydroxy 11-dehydrocorticos-terone hormone.

In public and governmental affairs, a succession of situations and events has been favorable to the development of acronyms. First there came the host of alphabetical agencies which were created in the early years of the Roosevelt administration and even before, some of which, like NRA and WPA, had a relatively short life; others, such as RFC and TVA, continue to play an important role in the national scene. The increase in labor organizations during this period contributed UAW, CIO, and many less widely known. Our entry into the Second World War gave rise to still others; most of us still recall OPA and WPB.

Military organization, both in the battle areas and in the staff room, vastly more complex than it had ever been before, furnished a host of coinages of almost incredible length: those of the SHAEF type and those of the COMINCH and CINCPAC varieties. Moreover, every one of the women's organizations auxiliary to the armed forces employed an acronym for ordinary reference; it will be necessary to mention only the WACS and the WAVES, but the tendency extended to the Marines and Coast Guard as well.

The United Nations also has a host of organizations with titles, necessarily long because of considerations of accuracy, which have been treated in the same way: WHO and UNESCO are among the most familiar. Up to the present, strangely enough, this tendency has been evident primarily upon a national and international level. It is indeed fortunate that each of the forty-eight states has not created its own multitude of terms. Had they done so, it would truly require a code book to get around the country.

The fraternal lodge provides another area, more or less peculiar to American life, where we find the initials of the somewhat grandiose and often cryptic titles of the organizations in frequent use, but with a slight difference. Such mysterious combinations as BPOE, KP, FOE, LOOM, AOH are familiar to millions of Americans, but except for KC, YMCA, and YWCA, they are rarely spoken. They tend to remain on a written level of the language.

In considering the final category of American word coinages, the creation or invention of high-sounding, mouth-filling words, it is necessary first to catch the spirit behind the process. This entails our looking a bit into American folklore and folk characters. Carl Carmer, in the foreword to his collection of such material, makes a very acute observation. He writes:

The people of almost every nation in the world except the
United States have liked to make up stories about 'the little
people.' Even the American Indians tell some beautiful tales
about them. But Americans have been so busy doing big jobs
that they have never taken time off to let their minds play
with the tiny folk who have magic powers. At the end of a
hard day's work the American cowboys or miners or lumber-
jacks or applepickers have had their fun out of making up
stories about men who could do jobs that could just not be
done, and in an impossibly short time with one hand tied
behind them. The dreams of American workers, naturally
enough, have never been delicate, exquisite, or polite—like
most fairy stories. They have been big and powerful, and a
strong wind is always blowing through them.

Carmer's last clause accounts for the title, *Hurricane's Children*,
that he gave to these stories of such American folk characters as
Paul Bunyan, Mike Fink, John Henry, Strap Buckner, and Steam-
boat Annie. All of these illustrate the typical exaggeration of the
frontiersman and his tales. Paul Bunyan could cut down two trees
with a single blow of a double-bladed axe, one with the down-,
and the other with the up-stroke. Strap Buckner used to knock
down bulls with a single blow of an iron pestle. Mike Fink could
jump across rivers; John Henry could carry a bale of cotton under
each arm and two on his head.

This frontier exaggeration found a verbal outlet in the 'tall
talk' characteristic not only of folk heroes but of real individuals
as well. One writer has painstakingly defined 'tall talk' as 'a form
of utterance ranging in composition from striking concoctions of
ingeniously contrived epithets expressing disparagement or en-
comium, to wild hyperbole, fantastic simile and metaphor, and a
highly bombastic display of oratory, employed to impress the lis-
tener with the physical prowess or general superiority of the
speaker.' This is an instance, however, where illustration is more
effective than definition, no matter how precise. Davy Crockett,
for example, describes himself as:

> . . . fresh from the back-woods, half horse, half alligator, a
> little touched with snapping turtle, can wade the Mississippi,

leap the Ohio, ride a streak of lightning, slide down a honey locust and not get scratched. I can whip my weight in wildcats, hug a bear too close for comfort, and eat any man opposed to Jackson.

The tendency toward high-flown simile is evident in the speech, purported to have been delivered by an Arkansas legislator in opposition to a proposal to change the name—actually the pronunciation of the name—of his state:

Compare the lily of the valley to the gorgeous sunrise; the discordant croak of the bullfrog to the melodious tones of a nightingale; the classic strains of Mozart to the bray of a Mexican mule; the puny arm of a Peruvian prince to the muscles of a Roman gladiator—but never change the name of Arkansas.

In addition to the braggadoccio and the highly figurative language there is evident a tendency toward the invention of high-sounding words. The frontiersman, ring-tailed roarer, half horse and half alligator, described himself as *kankarriferous* and *rambunctious*, his lady love as *angeliferous* and *splendiferous*. With consummate ease he could *teetotaciously exfluncticate* his opponent in a *conbobberation*, that is to say a conflict or disturbance, or *ramsquaddle* him *bodaciously*, after which the luckless fellow would *absquatulate*. He invented such fanciful animals as the *guyascutus* and the *ricaboo racker*. When deceived he was *hornswoggled*, when bewildered, *obfusticated*. Other terms of the same general nature which might be mentioned are *cahoots, catawampus, flusticated, jumpsecute, snollygoster, ripsniptious, slantindicular, helliferocious,* and *elegantiferously*.

There are two things to be observed about these mouth-filling words. Most of them first appear in print during the 'thirties and 'forties of the nineteenth century. The majority of them are built upon a very few suffixes: *-acious, -iferous, -ticate,* and *-icute* are prominent among them.

This tendency toward the bizarre creation is a significant feature of American English which can be accounted for in terms of cultural history and linguistic tradition. It stems, I believe, from the ornate diction of the Elizabethans, which is to be found in many writers of the period, but which was particularly evident in such a work as Marston's *Scourge of Villainy*. It was Marston whose outlandish vocabulary was satirized in Jonson's *Poetaster*.

In America this employment of the tumid and the turgid in vocabulary is to be seen in Nathaniel Ward's *The Simple Cobler of Aggawam* (1647), a work which has scarcely received the careful study that its vocabulary deserves. For example, in speaking of the possibility of religious liberty within a single province, he wrote: 'If the whole conclave of Hell can so compromise, exadverse and diametricall contradictions, as to compolitize such a multimonstrous manfrey of heteroclytes and quicquidlibets quietly; I trust I may say with all humble reverence, they can doe more then the Senate of Heaven.' And again in discussing women's fashions, the author's disapproval finds expression in the following:

> But when I heare a nugiperous Gentledame inquire what dresse the Queen is in this week; what the nudiustertian fashion of the Court; I mean the very newest: with egge to be in it in all haste, whatever it be; I look at her as the very gizzard of a trifle, the product of a quarter of a cypher, the epitome of nothing, fitter to be kick't, if shee were of a kickable substance, than either honour'd or humour'd.
>
> To speak moderately, I truly confesse, it is beyond the ken of my understanding to conceive, how those women should have any true grace, or valuable vertue, that have so little wit as to disfigure themselves with such exotick garbes, as not only dismantles their native lovely lustre, but transclouts them into gant bar-geese, ill-shapen-shotten-shell-fish, Egyptian Hyeroglyphicks, or at the best into French flurts of the pastery, which a proper English woman should scorne with her heels: it is no marvell they weare drailes on the hinder part of their heads, having nothing as it seems in the fore-part but a few Squirrils brains to help them frisk from one ill-favored fashion to another.

There can be no question about Ward's learning. Unusual as

his verbal creations were, they had been formed with a clear idea of the Latin and Greek meanings of their component parts. In England itself, similar stylistic tendencies on the part of such contemporaries of Ward as Burton and Sir Thomas Browne were overcome later in the seventeenth century by the restraining influences of the prose of Cowley and Dryden. That the verbally ornate continued in favor in America would seem to be indicated by the reprinting of Ward's work as late as 1713.

One may easily surmise that the admiration of the big word spread from the seacoast to the frontier, where new coinages now became a sport of the unlettered, fitting in neatly with the other hyperbolical characteristics of tall talk. To put it in another way, the Elizabethan tendency toward hyperbole or overstatement was, in this country, never submerged by the countermovement toward litotes, or understatement, which was a feature of the English classical revival of the late seventeenth and eighteenth centuries.

That the American of today still loves the mouth-filling phrase or word is illustrated by the alacrity with which Maury Maverick's coinage *gobbledygook* was adopted throughout the country in the closing years of the past decade. As a further example, witness the following statement reputedly used by the coach of the United States basketball team entered in the 1948 Olympic Games: 'We've got the world on the hip because American boys have the hucklety-buck and spizorinkum.'

The development of the second of these terms is worth noting as fairly typical of this type of coinage. It is derived from an impossible combination of Latin *specie* and *rectum*, 'the right kind,' and was used apparently in frontier areas during the mid-nineteenth century for 'hard' money as opposed to greenbacks or paper currency. It then acquired meanings as diverse as 'tireless energy' and 'tawdry adornment' and was used by no less a personage than the governor of one of our states in a recent election campaign. And while we are on the subject of politics, it would be well also to note the delight and curiosity occasioned by President Truman's revival of the term *snollygoster* in 1952. Its appearance sent inquiring reporters to the dictionaries and amateur etymologists to word lists of Pennsylvania Dutch.

The following dialogue from Lewis's *Elmer Gantry* is significant for its portrayal of what might be called the lay attitude toward the verbally esoteric:

> '. . . I' think I remember you as knee-high to a grasshopper. I suppose you study a lot of awful learned books now.'
> 'They make us work good and hard, Brother Jewkins. They give us pretty deep stuff: hermeneutics, chrestomathy, pericopes, exegesis, homiletics, liturgics, isagogics, Greek and Hebrew and Aramaic, hymnology, apologetics—oh, a good deal.'
> 'Well! I should *say* so!' worshipped old Jewkins, while Mrs. Gantry marveled to find Elmer even more profound than she had thought, and Elmer reflected proudly that he really knew what all but a couple of the words meant.

This will undoubtedly continue as a characteristic of American English for some time to come.

In the preceding chapter considerable space was given to those words which in American English have retained a meaning once current in England but which has since died out or changed there. Frequently, of course, the reverse occurred: new meanings were developed in this country, and many of these are traceable to the development of American institutions and American ways of life.

A familiar instance drawn from the vocabulary of college life is the word *fraternity*. The word is first recorded in English in 1330, applied to a religious order, and in 1386 to members of trade guilds and similar companies. The more strictly etymological meanings of brotherhood and brotherliness also appear in due course.

In this country within six months after the Declaration of Independence, a group of students at William and Mary College organized a literary society which they labeled cryptically with the three Greek letters Phi, Beta, and Kappa. The oath of membership pledged them to secrecy as to the significance of the name, to the pursuit of learning, and to eternal brotherhood. Because of this last, the organization became known as a fraternity. In due course similar societies followed, called themselves fraternities, and ultimately the term became definitely associated with collegiate organizations, social and professional as well as honorary, and even with similar groups in the secondary schools. The development of a specifically American institution gave the word a special application which it never acquired in England.

Nor did the process stop here. The development of women's colleges and of co-education gave rise to similar women's organizations; consequently a complementary specialization of the word *sorority* is to be found at the beginning of the present century, but even before this the term *fraternity*, despite its masculine derivational meaning, was extended to some women's groups, a number of which proudly retain it to this day.

As these societies developed traditions and modes of behavior, a whole new vocabulary grew up, bringing with it such further changes in meaning as are to be found in the terms *pledge, pledging*, and *rushing*—to say nothing of the phrase *pinning a girl*—such compounds as *fraternity pin, fraternity house, fraternity brother*, the clipped form *frat*, and the derivative *rushee*. A somewhat similar account might be written about the American development of fraternal orders as applied to groups which bear such startling names as Moose, Elks, Eagles, and Red Men.

Other instances of special meanings that developed partly as a result of conditions peculiar to American life are *sabbatical*, referring to a professorial holiday granted every seventh year, *corn*, applied specifically to maize rather than to grain in general, and *biscuit* for a small soft cake made with dough raised by either soda or baking powder.

Not infrequently words have acquired a broader meaning in the United States than they had in England. *Freight* offers an excellent example of this type of change. In England it is applied only to merchandise transported by water, and as such it bears a relationship to the word *fraught*, 'laden.' Early in the nineteenth century *freight* came to be applied in the United States to merchandise dispatched overland as well, quite possibly because long-distance shipping from one part of the country to another often involved hauling by land as well as by water. Transporting a load of goods from New York to St. Louis, for example, around 1840 might well have involved river packet, canal boat, short railroad hauls, and pack train.

Turning again to education, we find in the word *college* an excellent illustration of American generalization. The ancient colleges of Oxford and Cambridge were independent, self-governing societies or corporations within a university. In America *college* is often used as a term for the component departmental elements of a university (College of Medicine), and without qualification it regularly indicates an institution offering a four-year curriculum in the liberal arts. In this connection, we must remember that owing to the rapid expansion of educational facilities in this country, an institution which begins its existence as a liberal-arts college, or even with the first two years of such a curriculum, may within an incredibly short time add various types of professional training to its offerings and qualify as a university. Consequently, *college* has generally come to be used co-extensively with *university,* and 'going to college,' a purely American expression, may mean attending a university.

The word *pie* has also undergone an unusual series of developments in this country. In England it is still ordinarily used for baked meat or fish covered with a pastry crust. During the sixteenth century the term came to be applied to fruits prepared in the same way. It is this meaning in particular which seems to have come to America. To a speaker of British English, *pie* used without a qualifying term means a meat or fish pie; certainly the British child will never be as mystified as his American counterpart by the idea that the four-and-twenty blackbirds should have been baked into one. Conversely, only in America could the term *pieplant* have developed for the garden rhubarb.

As the art of pastry making developed in the United States, the open-faced pie and the meringue-covered pie replaced the earlier double-crusted pastry, again with a resultant change in meaning. Finally, the use of the term in *Eskimo Pie,* an oblong cut of ice cream entirely enclosed with a thin layer of chocolate, shows the complete obliteration of any association with pastry.

American politics, particularly in the rough-and-tumble days of Jacksonian democracy and the boss-ridden atmosphere of the post-Civil War era, appears to have given the word *politician* an unfavorable connotation. The *Oxford English Dictionary* definition of the term, satisfactorily explicit on this point, unconsciously reveals another British-American difference in terminology. It reads, 'One keenly interested in politics; one who engages in party politics or in political strife, or who makes politics his profession or business; also (especially in U.S.) in a sinister sense, one who lives by politics *as a trade*.'

It is safe to say that this contrast between a profession or business on the one hand and a trade on the other as a means of elucidating the less favorable meaning of *politician* in the United States would never have occurred to an American lexicographer. In fact, the definition invariably amuses any American who comes upon it simply because the hierarchy or ranking order which is implicit here has little significance in his scale of social values. It does serve as a reminder, however, that the verb *trade* in the sense of 'to shop' or 'to purchase regularly' (I always trade at Brown & Dobson's) is so purely American that it was not recorded by the *Oxford English Dictionary*, whose editorial staff and readers may well have been unaware of it, nor by the dictionaries of Americanisms, for whose editors it may have been so obvious and familiar that it was overlooked. It clearly developed out of the prevalence of bartering in a frontier society. As a final chapter, the widespread American practice of purchasing automobiles, refrigerators, washing machines, and other durable goods by turning in an older article of the same kind, usually in lieu of a down payment, has given rise to *trade-in*, used both as verb and noun.

Also in the realm of politics, the originally innocent term *junket* has undergone pejoration. The word originally meant a basket and first appears in English in 1382. A century later it was applied to a dessert of sweetened curds, then to any cake or

confection, and finally to a feast or banquet. From this last meaning, the verb *to junket* was created in the middle of the sixteenth
century. This verbal use apparently formed the basis of the American political term which means to take a trip at public expense,
ostensibly for purposes of legislative investigation or fact-finding,
for the verbal noun *junketing* is recorded as early as 1809, the
agentive *junketer* in 1862, and finally the noun itself in 1886.

Whereas *politician* and *junket* lost caste in American English
because of circumstances peculiar to the development of our institutions, certain other words have acquired less unfavorable
meanings. *Lumber* already discussed in connection with functional change, also serves as a striking instance of amelioration.
In England, *lumber* ordinarily indicates anything that takes up
room or is left lying about, and the lumber room in a house is
the one to which discarded toys, unwanted or unused wedding
presents, empty trunks and the like are relegated.

That this meaning was brought to America is evident from its
survival in some local dialects as well as from a good deal of
early legislation. The *Boston Records* for 1663 show that the inhabitants were cautioned to 'take care that noe wood, logges,
timber, stonnes, or any *other* lumber be layed upon the flatte to
the annoyance of any vesselles,' and a similar law was passed in
1701 against encumbering any street, lane, or alley. Certainly in
a pioneer community with building going on constantly, cut
timber would inevitably be piled in the streets from time to time,
and the circumstance that this was so often the offending impedi-
ment seems to have led to a specific association of *lumber* with
cut or milled wood, in contrast to uncut logs or possibly standing
trees, as is suggested by the report of Sir Edmund Andros, written in 1678: 'The Comodityes of the Country to ye westward are
wheat . . . pipe staves, timber, lumber & horses.' *Lumber* as a
noun meaning 'cut or milled logs' has given rise to a host of
compound formations.

The verb *haul* has similarly undergone a kind of amelioration
in American English. In England the word generally suggests a
considerable exertion of force or violence; in America it is used

very often as a synonym for *drawing* or *carting*. Whether pioneer conditions, particularly with respect to roads, made transportation so difficult that a great expenditure of force was necessary at all times, or whether the American tendency toward hyperbole tended to make a 'haul' of an ordinary carting task is difficult to say, but as early as 1714 we find a New Hampshire will stipulating, 'I give to my sons . . . all materials of iron for hauling, plowing, and such like.' Later on we find the word employed particularly in connection with railroad transportation and then apparently changing to a noun in the combination *long-* and *short-haul*, but it should be pointed out that British English developed *haulage* in this same connection as early as 1826.

This chapter has been devoted to developments in American English which took place because of the peculiar growth of American ways and institutions. Many of these were connected with life on the frontier of European civilization, and others bespeak a native ingenuity characteristic of our people, both those of original Anglo-Saxon stock and those who came here from non-English speaking countries.

The freedom with which certain English grammatical and lexical patterns were treated in America reflects this independence of spirit and lack of regard for accepted tradition. This is particularly evident in our many compound formations, our word blends, and our creation of mouth-filling terms. Certain changes, chiefly in meaning, have come about more gradually, and they too are new creations in a very real sense, answering to the slow but nevertheless inevitable development of American institutions and conditions under which the American people lived.

It is important, however, to realize that innovation, whether it is evidenced in the form of a word, its grammatical function, or its meaning, is but one of the processes which operated to make American English what it is today. Too often, in considerations of this general subject, innovation is stressed to the exclusion of other forces which are of equal significance but possibly somewhat less dramatic. Nor should we overlook the fact that the innovations which have been discussed in this chapter are almost totally confined to the area of the vocabulary. What is characteristically American in pronunciation is to be accounted for more often on the basis of the retention of older features of the language, and as we have already seen, departures from British English in inflection and syntax are relatively few. Yet the striking feature of American English innovations is their close correspondence to characteristics of the temperament and the ways of life of the people who developed them.

6

The Genteel Tradition and the Glorification of the Commonplace

P ervasive as the influence of the frontier may have been in early America, it was by no means all of one piece. Throughout most of the nineteenth century, settlement proceeded in stages. At the very time that the restless woodsman and trapper was making his initial foray into that portion of the wilderness farthest in advance of the march of civilization, the territory one or two hundred miles behind him was already taking on the aspects of permanent settlement. Farms were established in the oak openings or on the prairie; shipping points became the nuclei from which villages developed; local government, schools, churches, and even libraries soon took on at least a rudimentary form of organization. Even the theater and the lyceum course were seldom far behind the woodsman's axe. According to Constance Rourke:

> On rafts, in broadhorns, [theatrical] companies traveled down the Ohio and the Mississippi, stopping at the larger cities, often playing in small villages. Some went on by wagon into the hills of Kentucky, where the roads were so steep that they were obliged to unload their properties and carry them . . . Everywhere they found theaters or theaters were improvised for them; everyone came, black and white, children and their elders.

Certainly the reflection of frontier life and institutions, the absence of certain restraints associated with more permanent types of civilization, the ingenuity born of sheer necessity are all evident in the language. But there is more to the story than just this. Other ramifications of pioneer civilization and indeed certain counter-movements or reactions against it must be taken into consideration as well if we are to comprehend the development of American English in its totality.

One important factor in our early national life which had a profound effect on our language may appropriately be termed the glorification of the commonplace. It had its roots, perhaps, in two aspects of pioneer culture. First of all it must be realized that life in these primitive communities beyond the Appalachians was both hard and dull. Days were long; the work seemed endless. There were few comforts, and at times life must have seemed a continual struggle against cold and hunger. At the same time, many of the early pioneers had known other kinds of life. They had come from cities and towns which had acquired stability and certain cultural accoutrements. Small wonder, then, that the settlers permitted their imaginations to clothe their drab and commonplace surroundings with the salient features of the life they had known before.

One striking illustration of this tendency may be found in the peculiarly American development of the word *saloon*, the equivalent of British English *public house*. This word was originally an early eighteenth-century adaptation of French *salon*, and at the time it was borrowed signified just what it has continued to mean in French, namely, a drawing room. Not long after its adoption it came to be applied to drawing rooms which were particularly large and elegant, often those of a public character. This association with elegance and fashion has remained unchanged in British English—witness the coinage *saloon car* for an automobile with an enclosed body.

Moreover, late in the eighteenth or early in the nineteenth century there seems to have been some confusion in the terminology relative to establishments where liquor was sold at retail

or by the glass. *Tavern,* which in England came to denote a drinking place but one which had no sleeping accommodations in
connection, seems to have been used in America to designate a
hotel or inn. *Public house,* apparently used in America as early
as 1704 or at least in British legislation affecting American colonies, had become somewhat disreputable by including brothels
within the scope of its meaning. It was only natural, therefore,
that Americans should cast about for a new term which could
be respectably applied to a drinking establishment which was
not a hotel.

Their first coinage was *bar-room,* which is recorded by a
British traveler as early as 1809. Indirect evidence suggests that
the new term was insufficiently elegant to be wholly satisfactory,
nor did *groggery,* which appeared just a little later, seem to constitute an acceptable improvement. About three decades later we
find *saloon* appearing first on the eastern seaboard and then
spreading westward with amazing rapidity. Whether this was a
direct adaptation of the term in America, or whether its use was
first suggested by the English *saloon bar*—the most elegant of
the three types of bar in a public house, the other two being the
private and the public bar—cannot be determined from the evidence currently available. The important thing, however, is that
a word previously associated with fashion, elegance, and polite-
ness came to be used in connection with a kind of establishment
which was often fairly mean and dingy. Consequently the word
suffered in status, underwent pejoration.

As the agitation against the sale and use of alcohol increased,
the Anti-Saloon League was organized, and the saloon became a
symbol of corruption and evil influence. One of the principal
aims of the Prohibition movement was to wipe out the saloon,
and although it failed after a decade and a half, and liquor
eventually came back, Mencken's comment that, 'So far as I
know, there is not a simple undisguised saloon in the United
States today,' is still essentially correct. Nor is the owner of such
an establishment any longer content to refer to himself as a
saloonkeeper. The bartender, too, has attempted to cloak his

occupation with a new word, but the campaign, instituted in 1901 by the *Police Gazette*, to substitute *bar clerk* or *mixologist* as an occupational term had no success.

In all this, however, what is significant is the attempt to lend dignity and attractiveness through the use of a new and some- what elegant word—more elegant, perhaps, than the situation would reasonably permit.

A similar development occurred in connection with the term *opera house*, but unfortunately little factual information concern- ing its use is available in the usual lexicographical sources. Never- theless, throughout the nineteenth century and continuing on into the twentieth, it seems to have been customary in many small towns to use this word for the theater or auditorium which served the community. Some notion of its possible range of ap- plication may be obtained from Schlesinger and Fox's *History of American Life*; the time to which the quotation refers is 1870:

> Behind the courthouse grounds, around the corner from the Y.M.C.A. quarters and the Gazette office, stood the only other civic building—a barnlike brick structure sheltering the jail, the mayor's office, and an auditorium and stage. The "op'ry house" it was called by official decree.

Needless to say, most of the opera houses scattered throughout the length and breadth of the land seldom witnessed any per- formance even remotely resembling an opera, except possibly for an occasional venture into Gilbert and Sullivan by the local high school. The Lynds in their cultural analysis of Middletown [Muncie, Indiana] list the following as opera-house sensations of the 'nineties: *The Telephone Girl, Over the Garden Wall, East Lynne, Guilty Without Crime, The Black Crook*, and the inevit- able *Uncle Tom's Cabin*. It would seem, therefore, that *opera house* as a term for the small-town American theater represents precisely the same tendencies, cultural and semantic, that were behind the adoption of *saloon* for a drinking establishment: a desire to make the ordinary seem somewhat grander than it actually was, coupled perhaps with the hope that some day the structure might come to justify the name given to it.

Another manifestation of the same tendency is to be observed in connection with our terms for educational institutions and various types of training schools. In fact, there is if anything a double impulse here. The first is to be found in the tendency to dignify academic institutions of all kinds with a name that is a degree above, or at best somewhat more impressive than, that which they would merit in England. This has already been dealt with in part in connection with the generalization of the word *college*. A telling illustration of how this tendency operates is furnished by the state of Michigan where, in the decade of the 1930's, all but one of the normal schools in the state officially became Colleges of Education and in the 'fifties dropped the modifying phrase. This change was officially justified by the establishment in each of them of a liberal arts curriculum leading to the bachelor's degree, but the fact remains that *college* clearly seemed to the educational authorities a more desirable and respectable term than *school*. That *university* underwent a similar extension for much the same reason is evident from the exultant statement of a misguided patriot of the 1870's quoted by Schlesinger and Fox: 'There are two universities in England, four in France, ten in Prussia, and thirty-seven in Ohio.' Even *high school*, the American use of which dates from 1824, is seldom used for a secondary school in England, and in Europe it regularly denotes an institution of college or university rank. Here, however, American usage may have had its roots in Scotland.

The secondary tendency is to apply to trade schools and other establishments devoted to the training of artisans the same labels which have in the past been reserved for academic institutions. Again evidence is scanty, but *business college* as a term for a stenographic and secretarial training venture, is to be found as early as 1865. The dictionaries are strangely silent on *barber college*, but it was current in parts of the United States early in the twentieth century. Its sister institutions, the schools and colleges of cosmetology, devoted to initiating the beginner into the mysteries of the permanent wave, probably do not go back beyond the 1920's.

Occupational terminology in America has undergone a series of changes quite similar to those which have already been observed in connection with the educational institutions: old terms have been extended in application; new ones have been created. The words *doctor* and *professor* are obvious instances of extensions in application. Both of these are carefully restricted in their use in England, where surgeons are *Mr.* even if they do hold the M.D. degree, and professorships are naturally much less numerous than in the United States. In America, dentists, osteopaths, chiropractors, optometrists, chiropodists, and veterinarians are all doctors, and in addition the tremendous extension of the doctorate in American graduate schools, and the lavish manner in which American colleges and universities distribute honorary degrees add to the number of doctors on other levels as well. Even so, this does not take into account such jocular applications, either in full form or the clipped *Doc,* which, as the *Dictionary of Americanisms* indicates, was extended to logging camp cooks late in the nineteenth century.

Professor has developed in much the same direction; in fact, it may have begun earlier and gone farther. We find an enterprising bookseller styling himself a Professor of Book Auctioneering as early as 1774, and virtually every attempt at a glossary of Americanisms during the nineteenth century mentions the extension of the title to such groups as dancing teachers, magicians, and phrenologists. Certainly in most small towns the title was regularly applied not only to superintendents of school and principals but even to male grade-school teachers as well. The inevitable result of this wholesale doctoring and professoring is, of course, an avoidance of the titles by those who are normally entitled to them, an outcome suggested by the mock-serious society organized at the University of Virginia 'for the encouragement of the use of *mister* to all men, professional or otherwise.'

Academic usage in the north of the United States as contrasted with the south also offers a striking illustration of the operation of what might be called scarcity values. In the colleges and universities of the North there are many holders of the doctorate who have not yet attained professorial rank in a teaching faculty. Consequently, one who is both a professor and a doctor is customarily addressed as *professor*. In the South, on the other hand, until quite recently many college faculty members of professorial rank did not possess a doctor's degree. In this part of the country one who has both the rank and the degree is normally addressed as *doctor*.

In a sense the extension of the use of both *professor* and *doctor* is closely related to the American passion for honorifics, but a further discussion of these must be postponed until we take a hasty glance at the creation of other so-called professional titles and occupational terms. *Mortician,* frequently thought of in this connection, appears to have been created about 1895 on the convenient analogy of *physician,* and the same process of derivation has given us *beautician, loctician,* and six or eight others, all somewhat bizarre. It is possible that *mortician* may owe its creation quite as much to the age-old and constant search for euphemisms for terms connected with death and burial as to the desire for professional status. There is, after all, a somewhat gruesome pun in the word *undertaker,* and though it has served the English from 1698 on, they do at times soften the effect by substituting *funeral furnisher.*

Realtor, another oft-cited instance of the American creation of pseudo-professional terms, could be excused by the generously inclined on the ground that it permitted a single word to replace the somewhat cumbersome *real-estate agent,* but there is probably more truth than fiction in the sentiment expressed by Sinclair Lewis's Babbit to the effect that, 'We ought to insist that folks call us "realtors" and not "real-estate men." Sounds more like a reg'lar profession.' Though the Lewis citation comes from the early 'twenties, the term itself dates from 1915.

American regard for technology is shown by the overwhelming popularity of the word *engineer,* used in strange and numerous combinations. Our early use of the term in connection with railroading was a portent of things to come; the English in general content themselves with the somewhat more humdrum sounding *engine driver*. But since that time we have employed the word in an astounding number of combinations, running to well over 2000. H. L. Mencken reported that the Extermination Engineers, namely the rat and roach eradicators, have had a national association for some thirty years. Such further terms as *patent engineer, recreation engineer, erosion engineer,* and *casement window engineer* illustrate the variety of uses to which the term has been put.

The proposal of a Janitor's Institute, held at Mt. Pleasant, Michigan, in 1939, to the effect that janitors henceforth be called *engineer-custodians,* reveals as well the temporary nature of the satisfaction to be derived from verbal glorification, for historically *janitor* represents quite the same state of mind that gave rise to *realtor* and *mortician.* Derived somewhat artificially from the mythological character Janus, it was first used for a doorkeeper or porter, and its application to the sweeper of floors and builder of fires has been confined primarily to the United States; in England *caretaker* is the common term. As is evident from the action of the institute, even twenty years ago the word had become sufficiently tarnished that *engineer, custodian,* or both, sounded more attractive. One of the amusing sequels of the shift in terminology from *janitor* to *custodian* in one American university was that the title of the head of a research library had, in turn, to be changed from *Custodian* to *Director,* since there was some danger of confusing him with the janitor of the place.

Nor was the tendency to glorify the commonplace limited to the professional and work-a-day world. The American household bears some marks of this, even today. For example, the Lynds in their study *Middletown in Transition* find occasion to quote this very revealing excerpt from a current newspaper:

The time will easily be remembered when masculine and juvenile members of a household received glaring looks punctuated by lifted eyebrows when they forgot in the presence of

guests and referred to the evening meal as 'supper.' But time
has changed that. Smart folks are having buffet suppers, and
many . . .

Disregarding for the moment the recently regained prestige of
a certain type of supper, we may conclude that in the 'twenties
and 'thirties it was considered proper, particularly by women,
to refer to the evening meal as *dinner* and presumably to the
midday meal as *luncheon*, and that this terminology had quite
recently replaced *dinner* as the term for the noon meal and *supper* for the evening meal.

This shift is a slightly delayed reflection of the changed eating
habits of many American families which developed from the
increased urbanization and industrialization of American life,
and has, of course, some justification in fact. For the farming and
small-town families at the beginning of the present century,
the heaviest meal of the day was served at noon, and the evening
repast was considerably lighter. Thus for that time, *dinner* and
supper were accurate descriptions. The present tendency toward
lighter meals at noon, frequently consumed away from the home
by the male members of the family and by the children, has
resulted in the heavier meal being served at home in the evening,
with a resultant change in terminology and a prestige-loss for
supper.

In this connection it is interesting to observe that *supper* not
only continued in common use in America some sixty or seventy
years longer than in England, but that this was a matter for
comment by at least two mid-nineteenth century British travelers.
In 1859, Gosse in a series of letters from Alabama wrote, 'The
meal which we are accustomed to call "tea" is by Americans,
universally, I believe, called "supper," and it is the final meal,
there being but three in the day.' Five years later we find C.
Geithe reporting, 'I chatted . . . till tea, or as they called it,
supper.'

As American domestic architecture has changed, so too have
the names given to the various rooms. The principal phenomenon

over the past century has been the disappearance of a 'best room,' rarely occupied on weekdays, and used only to entertain guests and for holidays or festive occasions. In American usage this was the *parlor*. This in itself was a shift from British English, for there the term *parlor* was applied to a rather small intimate chamber, whereas the more pretentious one was called the *drawing room*, a term which never caught on with the Americans. In the United States, as long as the parlor was an institution, the room which was ordinarily used by the family circle was the *sitting room*, but as the parlor disappeared, the sitting room became the *living room*, and the former term came to be felt as somewhat rustic and old-fashioned.

It may be noted that only in America was the term *cuspidor* —an importation from Portuguese through Dutch—adopted for what was at one time a not uncommon accessory in the home, to say nothing of clubrooms and legislative halls. This somewhat delicate word was also introduced in England as early as 1781 but never gained any real currency.

Finally, the tendencies toward verbal elegance and senti-mentality appear to have combined to produce a more extensive use of *home* in America than in England. At the close of the last century, George Warrington Steevens commented, 'As to the home, the American talks about it a great deal. He never builds himself a house; he builds himself a home.' Consequently, con-tractors for domestic dwellings are *home builders*, the house-holder is a *homeowner*, vacuum sweepers, dishwashing machines, ironers, and the other manifold mechanical appurtenances of the American household are *home appliances*. School instruction in cooking and sewing has become *homemaking*, and when ex-alted to a more learned level, *home economics*. Even the house-wife became a *homemaker* by formal resolution of the Long Island Federation of Women's Clubs, as Mencken has pointed out. Moreover, the institutions of refuge for the needy and those of detention for troublesome juveniles are quite regularly *homes*, to say nothing of the *funeral home*, which now customarily serves as the setting for final rites.

Travelers to America, almost from its very beginning as an independent country, have taken great delight in pointing out what seemed to them a fundamental inconsistency between the theory of equality upon which the government of the country is based and the fondness of the American people for titles of honor. Although Crèvecœur, reflecting on his pre-Revolutionary experience, stoutly insisted that *lawyer, merchant,* and *farmer* were the fairest titles our country at that time afforded, observers from the 1840's on have a quite different story to tell. As late as 1896, George Warrington Steevens inquired somewhat petulantly in describing the American, 'Why does he cling all his life to the title of some rank or office he held twenty years ago?' Two answers to the question were offered some years before Steevens phrased it, and without question there is some truth in each. In 1849 the Scotsman Alexander Mackay defended the Americans on the ground that, 'the fondness for titles which they display is but a manifestation of the fondness for distinction natural to the human mind.' A somewhat different opinion was voiced a decade later by Thomas Colley Grattan, who concluded, 'Were a well-established national self-reliance felt among the leading men in the United States, there would be none of the melancholy parodies of "High Life," none of the yearnings after aristocratical distinctions which are now so flagrant.'

When American honorifics are examined in a dispassioned light, it must be said that they are still a far cry from Teutonic usage, for example. They are notable chiefly for some extension of such bogus military titles as *Colonel,* the retention of legislative and judicial titles, as noted by Steevens, beyond the period of service, and the somewhat comic extension of the word *Honorable* itself. Judged by either general European or Latin American standards in these matters, the English-speaking American becomes almost a shrinking violet. It is only in the light of English practice that our use of honorifics seems somewhat overweighted, and even the English have their silly periods, as anyone who witnessed the furor over the proper application and meaning of *Esquire* which raged in the autumn of 1953 can well testify.

In this connection it is well to remember that the United States came into being as the result of a political rather than a social revolution. The latter frequently does result in a highly conscious effort to do away with artificial titular distinctions; witness the adoption of *Citizen* in the French Revolution and that of *Comrade* in post-revolutionary Russia. This did not occur in the United States, for there was no nobility to displace, no class of governing officials to turn out of office. If anything, some offices and distinctions had to be created, and even the title to be given to the chief executive of the country was for a time a moot question.

In consequence of H. L. Mencken's picturesque and entertaining assault upon *Honorable,* little remains to be said except to point out the problem posed by the vastness of the country and the complexities of its governmental machinery. To begin with, we have the President and the members of his cabinet and the justices of the Supreme Court. No one would be inclined to doubt that any one of these merits the term. But if the executive and judicial branches of our government are thus entitled to the distinction, and so far we have imaginarily conferred it upon no more than thirty individuals, our very concept of the equality of all three branches of our government demands that all members of the Senate and the House of Representatives receive it as well. Thus at a single stroke we have added some 550 *Honorables.* Going back to the executive and judicial branches, we must now ask whether we stop with Supreme Court justices and cabinet secretaries. What about appellate and district judges, to say nothing of undersecretaries and assistant secretaries? There is the whole diplomatic corps in addition, and officials in special governmental agencies not represented in the cabinet.

Leaving the national government and pursuing the same problem on the state level, we must now multiply by forty eight the possibly 2000 *Honorables* we have already conferred. Nor can we stop here, for surely a metropolitan mayor has a position equal in dignity and responsibility to the governor of one of our smaller states. Ultimately we arrive at the township justice and the

village fire marshal. Moreover, many of these offices are no longer
than a biennium in duration, and once a man has acquired the
title he is not likely to relinquish it. The wonder is that anyone
at all escapes the term, or perhaps that we have not attempted
to create distinctions within it, that is to say, degrees and classi-
fications of honorability.

A further sector of the American vocabulary which scarcely
has a counterpart in British life comprises the wide variety of
names given to fraternal orders. The last two decades of the nineteenth century gave rise to an almost unbelievable number of
these, very nearly 500, in fact. Schlesinger and Fox, in commenting upon this gaudy variety, among which are included such
choice items as the American Order of Druids, the Prudent
Patricians of Pompeii, and the Concatenated Order of Hoo-Hoo,
make the very sound observation that 'the nomenclature of fra-
ternalism will someday offer interesting material for the student
of suppressed desires and wishful thinking.' Although they do
not develop the point, there can be little question that the
motivating force behind these is of a class with what we have
just observed.

Euphemism, verbal prudery or the avoidance of the unpleasant
word, is another somewhat indirect product of the frontier
which, from a semantic and lexical point of view at least, is
often closely allied to verbal glorification. In fact, it is often
difficult to decide whether the motive behind such a substitution
as that of *casket* for *coffin* was primarily that of suggesting something more elegant or that of avoiding a term connected with
death and burial. Much of the verbal prudery, however, for
which we became notorious in the nineteenth century, may be
traced to two factors: the position of woman in American society
and the predominantly middle-class character of American culture.

The second of these points is so obvious as not to require
extensive elaboration. Within the history of modern societies it
has always been the middle class which has manifested a greater
and more anxious concern for the proprieties than either the

lower class, which has tended toward indifference, or the upper, which has been protected by a thick coat of self-assurance. Among the proprieties thus affected, that of language has usually assumed a prominent position. It was the English middle class, or at least the upper sector of it, which created the demand that led to the excessive schoolmastering of the language in eighteenth-century England. That the Puritan settlers of New England—also predominantly middle class—were intensely concerned with linguistic propriety is indicated by the amount of colonial legislation directed against profanity. Noah Webster interested himself in expurgating the Bible, and considered this one of his important works. There is ample evidence in a dozen sociological studies that most Americans today are prone to think of themselves as belonging to the middle class. Consequently, there is every reason to expect from American English a typical middle-class delicacy, expressed in a multitude of linguistic taboos. The record, as we shall see, in no way dispels our expectations.

This verbal delicacy received a strong reinforcement from the position which women enjoyed in our frontier society. In his *Society and Thought in Early America,* Harvey Wish points out that:

> . . . their relative scarcity and economic opportunities made them more difficult to please in courtship. While the South enjoyed a latter-day chivalry with roots deep in feudal times, the North, too, had its ritual of courtesies due to women. Everywhere seduction and breach of promise suits were apt to be prejudiced in the woman's favor. Here one addressed a mixed audience as 'Ladies and Gentlemen' instead of the traditional 'Gentlemen and Ladies.' Women travelled alone without losing caste, and their daughters dispensed with chaperones (even if they belonged to the well-to-do class). While the Industrial Revolution was emancipating western European women as well as their American sisters, the American woman was definitely ahead in status.

Because of this scarcity value, American women seem to have been in a position to foster an extreme sensitivity in linguistic matters. Calhoun in his study of the American family cites one letter written a few years before 1850 which asserts, 'Women can alter the dialect, change the manners, dictate the dress and habits of life, and control the morals of every community.' Captain Frederick Marryatt's comments on this point have furnished what is often considered the classic example of verbal delicacy. He tells first of how he offended an American woman by saying *legs* instead of limbs and then goes on to the account of the girls' seminary where the piano 'limbs' were 'dressed in modest little trousers with frills at the bottom of them.' That the veracity of the latter story has been questioned is of little importance; it is true in spirit to the segment of American life it purported to reflect. Nor was this cult of super-refinement one of short duration only. The Lynds in their study of Middletown cite a commencement essay at the local high school as late as 1891 bearing the title, 'Woman is Most Perfect When Most Womanly.'

The first and most prominent linguistic effect of female dominance and middle-class morality was an extreme reticence on matters directly or even remotely connected with sex. Again the Lynds' *Middletown in Transition* furnishes corroborative evidence from a society studied less than two decades ago:

> Sex is one of the things Middletown has long been taught to fear. Its institutions—with the important exception of the movies and some of the periodicals it reads, both imported from the outside culture—operate to keep the subject out of sight and out of mind as much as possible.

In language, of course, questionable subjects are kept out of sight and mind, ostensibly if not actually, by developing new and less shocking terms to replace those which have taken on taboo characteristics. All languages do this to some extent. It is the degree to which these euphemistic tendencies have operated in American English that is of particular interest.

One outlet for verbal delicacy of this nature was the creation of a host of more or less thinly disguised terms for houses of prostitution. *Assignation house* is cited by the *Dictionary of Amer-*

icanisms for 1854; *house of assignation* preceded this by twenty years. *Sporting house,* which in England meant first merely a house frequented by sportsmen and later a gambling house, was finally applied to a brothel in America in 1894 in a book which bore the somewhat disconcerting title, *If Christ Came to Chicago.* None of the dictionaries, however, seem to record the related use of *sport* for a prostitute, which was current about the same time. *Crib* also reflects the same transition from a gaming house to one of prostitution, though somewhat earlier, and such terms as *cat house, fancy house, cow bag,* and *call house* were all in use at one time or another; and on a somewhat more dignified level, *disorderly house* and *house of ill fame. Cadet* as a euphemism for procurer seems to have flourished from the first to the third decades of the twentieth century. There was also an equal reticence with respect to naming specific venereal diseases, but this has been generally overcome within the past twenty years.

Another object which has particularly invited euphemistic terminology is what the English call a *water closet* and the Americans a *toilet.* Commenting on the use of *toilet,* the *Oxford English Dictionary* says, 'In the U.S. especially a dressing room furnished with bathing facilities; in a restricted sense, a bathroom, a lavatory,' but it is difficult to fix the time when the precise application to the water closet itself occurred. The first citation which may be so interpreted with reasonable certainty bears the date 1909, though it must have had this meaning considerably earlier. *Rest room* (1909) and *comfort station* (1904) were also concocted during the first decade of the century, and Mencken credits *powder room* to the speakeasies of the Prohibition era. The American use of *washroom* in the same sense goes back to 1853.

It is to be expected that during a period of extreme verbal delicacy there will be many taboos for various parts of the body, particularly those which have any connection with sex or with the excretive functions. Mid-nineteenth-century America was no exception. This topic, however, has been so fully treated by

Mencken and by Pyles that it will be necessary only to point out one or two matters which seem to have been overlooked.

For example, despite Captain Marryatt's oft-quoted stories of the woman who was offended at the mention of *limb*, it should not be forgotten that this word acquired the meaning of 'leg' not in America but in England as early as 1400. *Oxford English Dictionary* citations show that it was in constant use in England from the beginning of the fifteenth century until 1837. Marryatt's account of his American experience bears the date 1839, and from that time until 1924 all the citations are American. What we have here then is the continuation of a British euphemism rather than an American invention.

The taboo against *leg* was extended to fowl prepared for the table, as is frequently pointed out, but *drumstick*, one of the euphemisms which appeared on the scene as a substitute, is clearly of British origin, and on the basis of dictionary evidence, at least, was as much used in Britain as in the United States. The extension of *joint* from its British use in connection with such meats as beef, mutton, and venison, to roast fowl seems clearly to have originated in America, and so too the further distinction between a first joint and a second. An English traveler in America in 1845 reported himself as being 'requested by a lady, at a public dinner table, to furnish her with the first and second joint.' The presumed indecency of the word *leg*, coupled with an almost equally strong taboo against *breast*, gave rise to another pair of American euphemisms used in this connection. Thomas C. Grattan, in his *Civilized America* (1859) explained that, 'some . . . would scarcely hesitate, though almost all call it the "white meat," in contradistinction to the "dark meat" as all ladies and gentlemen designate the legs of poultry.' *White meat* as a term had previously existed in England, but was limited in its meaning to milk, cheese, and other dairy products, literally white food.

Undergarments for both men and women likewise offered a fertile field for mid-nineteenth-century ingenuity. *Unmentionables*, which refers at times to trousers and at others to drawers, is cited as early as 1839; *sub-trousers* as late as 1890. Between these dates a wide variety of terms appeared, though it should be noted that *inexpressibles,* sometimes classed with American euphemisms of this type, is actually British in origin and seems to have been used in England throughout the greater part of the century.

Death, dying, and burial constitute another area of the lexicon in which most languages develop a large number of euphemisms. America was no exception, and Professor Louise Pound has dealt with this subject most exhaustively. Of the American terms which developed in this way, I have already mentioned one of the best known and most widely used today: *casket,* which serves as a delicate substitute for *coffin.* It seems to have entered the language by way of the compound *burial casket,* which along with *burial case* was coined in the 'fifties and 'sixties of the last century. It must have caught on very rapidly, for by 1870 a British news correspondent in New York was able to make the flat statement, 'In America a coffin is called a casket.' That the term did not immediately win universal favor is shown by Nathaniel Hawthorne's comment in *Our Old Home* (1863): ' "Caskets!"—a vile modern phrase which compels a person . . . to shrink . . . from the idea of being buried at all.' The perfumed practices of the modern mortician have, of course, resulted in a host of evasive expressions, against which Evelyn Waugh trained the shafts of his wit in the novel *The Loved One.*

The Puritan prohibition of profanity has already been mentioned, and although the number of violations of their laws clearly indicates that this was more often honored in the breach than in the observance, yet the fact that the laws should have existed at all, as well as the length of time they remained on the books, offers satisfactory evidence of an active taboo against profanity in the Puritan conscience. As a consequence of this, it would seem, American English has developed a whole lexicon of near-swearing, including *darn, drat, doggone, blasted, Sam Hill, gee whittaker, gee whiz,* and their progeny of sixty or seventy others, most of them still bearing more or less phonetic resemblance to the particular morsel for which they have been substituted.

Darn offers a fairly satisfactory example of the way one of these terms developed. We need not concern ourselves here with the debate which went on some years ago over whether *derne,* the Middle English word for 'secret,' was its real progenitor, or whether it emanated from an aphetic form of *eternal,* with the *er* pronounced as in British *clerk* (*clark*). The facts are simply that we do have *darnation* used as an adjective as early as 1798, and a quarter of a century later as an interjection. The earliest examples indicate use by, or with reference to, coastal New Englanders. If we assume that by this time post-vocalic *r* was either weakened or had disappeared entirely, and that the coastal New England *a* before *r* was a low central vowel with something of the quality of present-day Bostonian *park* [pa:k], the close resemblance of this to the ordinary pronunciation of *damnation* is clear enough. They are virtually the same except for the medial *m*. *Darn* appears by itself a decade or so later. A contemporary but very shrewd and accurate analysis of the whole situation was given in 1832 by J. T. Buckingham, writing in the *New England Magazine*: 'We have "Gaul darn you" for "G— d— you" . . . and other like creations of the union of wrath and principle.'

Nor is it merely the nineteenth century and the standards of propriety peculiar to it which give the impetus to usages designed to soften the harsh facts of life. We have at hand at least one twentieth-century phenomenon which has fostered a similar development—present-day American educational practices. The extension of elementary and secondary education to virtually all of the youth population, coupled with the determination on the part of educational psychologists to avoid injury to budding juvenile or adolescent personalities, no matter how academically inept, has resulted on the one hand in almost a total abandonment of the practice of failing a student, thus causing him to repeat a grade or unit of work, and on the other, in the creation of a host of special courses designed for those who are clearly unfitted for even the watered-down academic regimen of the present era. Consequently the practice of advancing the academic failures has become known as *social promotion* in some quarters, and high-school curricula now include courses which bear such strange labels as *Social English* and *Social Mathematics*. Moreover, the 'exceptional' child may mean one of less than normal intelligence.

It is important to recognize that taboos and the resulting euphemisms have always operated in language. We have had them in English from the time that some Anglo-Saxon monk with an over-keen sense of propriety, coupled with a distinctly worldly knowledge of what went on in harbor resorts, coined the term *port-cwene* (port woman) to translate 'harlot' in the parable of the Prodigal Son, up to the present era when one of our recent governmental administrations was careful to characterize a slight economic depression as a *recession*. The interesting aspect of the mid-nineteenth-century development of euphemisms in America lies in the peculiar combination of cultural circumstances which brought it about, the lavish scale upon which it operated, and the extremes which it often attained.

Every movement has its counter-force, and the genteel tradition of the past was no exception. Nineteenth-century America was not without those individuals who not only accepted their lack of culture and refinement as an established fact but who gloried in it, and indeed flaunted it. The 'I don't know anything about art but I know what I like' cliché—and the attitude it portrays—is a patent instance of this resistance to culture with a capital *C*. There is a good deal of this, for example, in Mark Twain, some of it undoubtedly sincere and some clearly with tongue in cheek. The extreme of such an attitude has at times been called the 'mucker pose,' one which certain politicians and others dependent upon large-scale popular support have at times found it profitable to adopt. Linguistically the mucker pose is frequently manifested by the conscious employment of features of substandard English. A case in point was the thoroughly cul-

tured millionaire candidate for the presidential nomination recently, who rarely made a speech or television appearance
without using *ain't* at least once. Currently this is scarcely a
potent factor on the linguistic scene, but it is present to some
extent, and its existence cannot be overlooked.

7

Regional and Social Variations

The English language is spoken natively in America by no less than 145 million persons over an area of some three million square miles. Various parts of the United States differ considerably from each other with respect to climate, topography, plant and animal life, economic conditions, and social structure. Sociologists and historians recognize at least six regional cultures within the continental borders of the country. The same a priori grounds that led us to assume the existence of a series of differences between British and American English at the outset of this work will justify the inference that the language is likely not to be uniform throughout the country. The American novelist John Steinbeck in his *Grapes of Wrath* offers convincing evidence of the plausibility of this assumption:

> 'I knowed you wasn't Oklahomy folks. You talk queer kinda— That ain't no blame, you understan'.'

> 'Ever'body says words different,' said Ivy. 'Arkansas folks says 'em different, and Oklahomy folks says 'em different. And we seen a lady from Massachusetts, an' she said 'em differentest of all. Couldn' hardly make out what she was sayin'.'

Early travelers to America and native commentators on the language agree on the existence of regional differences at an

131

early period in our national history. Mrs. Anne Royal called attention to various Southernisms in the works which she wrote during the second quarter of the nineteenth century, and as early as 1829, Dr. Robley Dunglison had identified many of the Americanisms, in the glossary he compiled, with particular portions of the country. Charles Dickens recognized regional differences in the English he encountered in his first tour of the United States, and William Howard Russell, reporting on Abraham Lincoln's first state banquet, at which he was a guest, mentions his astonishment at finding 'a diversity of accent almost as great as if a number of foreigners had been speaking English.'

A number of other observers, however, were sufficiently impressed by the uniformity of the language throughout the country to make this a matter of comment. De Tocqueville, in a rather extended treatment of the language of the young republic, flatly declared, 'There is no patois in the New World,' and John Pickering, along with Noah Webster easily the most distinguished of our early philologists, also remarked on the great uniformity of dialect through the United States, 'in consequence,' as he said, 'of the frequent removals of people from one part of our country to another.'

There is truth in both types of comment. People in various parts of the United States do not all speak alike, but there is greater uniformity here than in England or in the countries of Western Europe, and this makes the collection of a trustworthy body of information upon the regional variations in American English a somewhat difficult and delicate matter.

The gathering of authentic data on the dialects of many of the countries of Western Europe began in the latter decades of the nineteenth century. The *Atlas linguistique de la France* followed closely upon the heels of the *Sprachatlas des deutschen Reichs,* and the activities of the English Dialect Society were initiated about the same time. In 1889 a group of American scholars organized the American Dialect Society, hoping that the activities of this organization might result in a body of material from which either a dialect dictionary or a series of linguistic maps, or both, might be compiled. The society remained relatively small, however, and although some valuable information appeared in its journal *Dialect Notes,* a systematic survey of the regional varieties of American English has not yet resulted from its activities.

The past quarter of a century, however, has seen the development of such a survey. Beginning in 1928, a group of researchers under the direction of Professor Hans Kurath, now of the University of Michigan, undertook the compilation of a *Linguistic Atlas of New England* as the first unit of a projected *Linguistic Atlas of the United States and Canada.* The New England atlas, comprising a collection of some 600 maps, each showing the distribution of a single language feature throughout the area, was published over the period from 1939 to 1943. Since that time, field work for comparable atlases of the Middle Atlantic and of the South Atlantic states has been completed, and the materials are awaiting editing and publication. Field records for atlases of the North Central states and the Upper Middle West are virtually complete, and significant beginnings have been made in the Rocky Mountain and the Pacific Coast areas. Surveys in Louisiana, in Texas, and in Ontario are also under way. It is perhaps not too optimistic to predict that within the next twenty-five years all of the United States and Canada as well will have been covered in at least an initial survey.

For a number of reasons it is not easy to collect a body of valid and reliable information on American dialects. The wide spread of education, the virtual extinction of illiteracy, the extreme mobility of the population—both geographically and from one social class to another—and the tremendous development of a number of media of mass communication have all contributed to the recession of local speech forms. Moreover, the cultural insecurity of a large portion of the American people has caused them to feel apologetic about their language. Consequently, they seldom display the same degree of pride or affection that many an English or a European speaker has for his particular patois. Since all dialect research is essentially a sampling process, this means that the investigator must take particular pains to secure representative and comparable samples from the areas which are studied. Happily, the very care which this demands has had the result of developing the methodology of linguistic geography in this country to a very high level.

In general, the material for a linguistic atlas is based upon the natural responses of a number of carefully selected individuals representing certain carefully chosen communities, which in themselves reflect the principal strains of settlement and facets of cultural development in the area as a whole. Since the spread of education generally results in the disappearance of local or regional speech forms, and since the extension of schooling to virtually all of the population has been an achievement of the past seventy-five years, it became necessary for the American investigator to differentiate between the oldest generation, for whom schooling beyond the elementary level is not usual, and a middle-aged group who is likely to have had some experience with secondary schools. In addition, it is highly desirable to include some representatives of the standard or cultivated speech in each region, that their language may serve as a basis of comparison with the folk speech. Accordingly, in the American atlases, from each community represented, the field worker will choose at least two, and sometimes three representatives, in con-trast to the usual practice of European researchers, who may safely content themselves with one. Moreover, it is equally neces-sary to make certain that the persons chosen in any community have not been subject to alien linguistic influences; consequently, only those who have lived there all of their lives, and preferably those who represent families who have long been identified with the area in question, are interviewed, although as one moves westward into the more recently settled areas this is not always possible.

Since complete materials are available only for the eastern seaboard and for the area north of the Ohio River as far west as the Mississippi, tentative conclusions relative to the regional variations in American English can be presented only for the eastern half of the country. The principal dialect areas presented in Kurath's *Word Geography of the Eastern United States,* are indicated on the accompanying map.

The three major dialect boundaries, it will be noted, cut the country into lateral strips and are labeled by Professor Kurath *Northern, Midland,* and *Southern* respectively. The line which separates the Northern and Midland areas begins in New Jersey a little below Sandy Hook, proceeds northwest to the east branch of the Susquehanna near Scranton, Pennsylvania, then goes westward through Pennsylvania just below the northern tier of counties. In Ohio the boundary dips below the Western Reserve, then turns northwest again, passing above Fort Wayne, Indiana. When it approaches South Bend it dips slightly to the southwest and cuts through Illinois, reaching the Mississippi at a point slightly above Quincy. The other principal boundary, that separating the Southern and Midland areas, begins at a point somewhat below Dover in Delaware, sweeps through Baltimore in something of an arc, turns sharply southwest north of the Potomac, follows the crest of the Blue Ridge in Virginia, and south of the James River swerves out into the North Carolina Piedmont. As we approach the lower part of South Carolina and Georgia the boundary is as yet unknown.

Even these necessarily incomplete results of the survey carried on under Professor Kurath and his associates have modified considerably our previous conceptions of the regional distribution of American speech forms. This modification is brought about principally by adding one concept and eliminating another. The concept thus eliminated has been variously known as Middle Western, Western, or General American. The older view of American dialects, reduced to its simplest terms, recognized the existence of a New England type of speech, a Southern type, and the remainder was generally blanketed by some such term as General American.

It seems clear now that what is neither New England nor Southern—which includes, of course, something between three-quarters and nine-tenths of the continental United States—is far

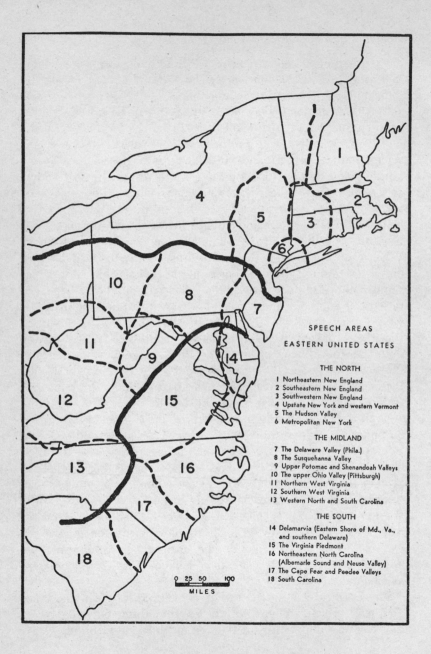

SPEECH AREAS

EASTERN UNITED STATES

THE NORTH

1 Northeastern New England
2 Southeastern New England
3 Southwestern New England
4 Upstate New York and western Vermont
5 The Hudson Valley
6 Metropolitan New York

THE MIDLAND

7 The Delaware Valley (Phila.)
8 The Susquehanna Valley
9 Upper Potomac and Shenandoah Valleys
10 The upper Ohio Valley (Pittsburgh)
11 Northern West Virginia
12 Southern West Virginia
13 Western North and South Carolina

THE SOUTH

14 Delamarvia (Eastern Shore of Md., Va., and southern Delaware)
15 The Virginia Piedmont
16 Northeastern North Carolina (Albemarle Sound and Neuse Valley)
17 The Cape Fear and Peedee Valleys
18 South Carolina

0 25 50 100
MILES

too diverse and lacking in homogeneity to be considered a single major dialect. We know, for example, that there are a significant number of differences, both in vocabulary and in verb inflections, between the folk speech of most of Pennsylvania and that of New York state, and between Michigan and Wisconsin on the one hand, and most of Indiana and large portions of Illinois and Ohio on the other. As our information for the rest of the country becomes available, there can be little doubt that this conclusion will be strengthened.

The concept which has been added is the recognition of a Midland type of speech as distinct from both North and South. An examination of the evidence which Professor Kurath presents in his *Word Geography* leaves no doubt that the speech of this area, though it is by no means uniform, is sufficiently differentiated from both North and South to justify its classification as a major dialect area. This conclusion is supported not only by Atwood's study of the verb forms in the eastern portion of the country but by the available materials from the North Central States.

The map shown on page 136 includes also a few, but not all, of the sub-dialect areas which merit recognition. In the North the principal area is that which separates coastal New England from western New England, New York state, and the territory to the west. In general, this boundary follows the line of the Green Mountains, the Berkshire Hills, and the Connecticut River. The Metropolitan New York area consists of a broad circle with the city itself at the center; the Hudson Valley area encompasses the original Dutch settlements in New York and northern New Jersey, spreading into northeastern Pennsylvania. The Midland area is divided into northern and southern sub-areas, the line of demarcation being just a little south of the Old National Road in Ohio, Indiana, and Illinois. Within the Southern dialect region, the Virginia Piedmont and the Delmarva peninsula constitute distinct sub-areas.

Thus far it is the lexical materials gathered in connection with the various atlas projects which have been analyzed most ex-

tensively, and as the title of Professor Kurath's work indicates,
his plotting of the major dialect areas is based upon vocabulary
evidence. For example, characteristic Northern expressions that
are current throughout the area include *pail, swill, whiffletree* or
whippletree, comforter or *comfortable* for a thick quilt, *brook,
co-boss* or *come-boss* as a cow call, *johnnycake, salt pork,* and
darning needle for a dragonfly. In the Midland area we find
blinds for roller shades, *skillet, spouting* or *spouts* for eaves, a
piece for food taken between meals, *snake feeder* for a dragonfly,
sook as the call to calves, *armload* for an armful of wood; and
one *hulls* beans when he takes off the shells. A quarter *till* the
hour is a typical Midland expression, as is the elliptical *to want
off,* or *out,* or *in.* The South has *lightwood* as the term for
kindling, a *turn* of wood for an armful; stringbeans are generally
snap beans; hasslet is the term for the edible inner organs of a
pig, *chittlins* for the small intestine; and in this area cows are
said to *low* at feeding time.

The sub-dialect areas also have their characteristic forms. In
coastal New England, for instance, *pigsty* is the normal term for
pig-pen, *bonny clapper* for curdled sour milk, *buttonwood* for a
sycamore, and *pandowdy* for a cobbler type of dessert. Eastern
Virginia has *cuppin* for a cowpen, *corn house* for a crib. *Lumber
room* survives as the term for a storeroom. A grasshopper is
known as a *hopper grass,* and *batter bread* is used for a soft
cornbread containing egg.

As far as the sectors of the American lexicon which reflect
regional differences are concerned, the matter is trenchantly
summarized in Kurath's *Word Geography,* where the author
points out first of all that the vocabularies of the arts and sciences,
of industries, commercial enterprises, social and political institutions, and even many of the crafts, are national in scope because
the activities they reflect are organized on a national basis. He
then goes on to say:

> Enterprises and activities that are regionally restricted have,
> on the other hand, a considerable body of regional vocab-

ulary which, to be sure, may be known in other parts of the country, even if it is not in active use. The cotton planter of the South, the tobacco grower, the dairy farmer, the wheat grower, the miner, the lumberman, and the rancher of the West have many words and expressions that are strictly regional and sometimes local in their currency.

Regional and local expressions are most common in the vocabulary of the intimate everyday life of the home and the farm— not only among the simple folk and the middle class but also among the cultured . . . Food, clothing, shelter, health, the day's work, play, mating, social gatherings, the land, the farm buildings, implements, the farm stocks and crops, the weather, the fauna and flora—these are the intimate concern of the common folk in the countryside, and for these things expressions are handed down in the family and the neighborhood that schooling and reading and a familiarity with regional or national usage do not blot out.

It is not only in the vocabulary that one finds regional differences in American speech. There are pronunciation features as well. Throughout the Northern area, for example, the distinction between [o] and [ɔ] in such word pairs as *hoarse* and *horse*, *mourning* and *morning* is generally maintained; [s] regularly occurs in *grease* (verb) and *greasy*, and *root* is pronounced by many with the vowel of *wood*. Within the Northern area such sub-dialects as coastal New England and Metropolitan New York also show many characteristic forms; the treatment of the vowel of *bird* is only one of these, and words of the *calf, pass, path, dance* group constitute another. In the Midland area speakers fail to distinguish between *hoarse* and *horse*. Rounding is characteristic of the vowels of *hog, frog, log, wasp* and *wash*, and in the last of these words an *r* often intrudes in the speech of the not too highly educated. The vowels of *due* and *new* will resemble that of *food* rather than *feud*. In the South, *r* is 'lost' except before vowels, as it is in eastern New England and New York City but not in the Northern area generally. Words like *Tuesday, due,* and *new* have a y-like glide preceding the vowel, and final [z] in *Mrs.* is the normal form.

Among the older, relatively uneducated group and even to some extent among the middle-aged informants who have had some secondary schooling there are also regional differences in inflectional forms and syntax. For example, *hadn't ought* for 'oughtn't,' *see* as a past tense form, *clim* for 'climbed' among the oldest sector of the population, *wan't* for 'wasn't,' *be* in such expressions as *How be you?*, and the choice of the preposition *to* in *sick to his stomach* are all characteristic of the Northern area. *Clum* for 'climbed,' *seen* for 'saw,' *all the further* and *I'll wait on you* are to be found in the Midlands, whereas *belongs to be*, *heern* for 'heard,' *seed* as the past tense of 'to see,' *holp* for 'helped,' *might could* and *mought have* are characteristic of the South.

All of this raises the question as to how the regional forms of American English developed in our three and one-half centuries of linguistic history. The first factor which must be taken into account is settlement history. Where did our earliest settlers come from, and what dialects did they speak? It was pointed out in Chapter 2 that at the time of the earliest settlements, English local and regional dialects were in a stronger position than they are today in that they constituted the natural speech of a greater portion of the English-speaking population and were in customary use farther up the social scale.

Moreover, it is quite unlikely that any single local settlement, even at the outset, ever consisted entirely of speakers of the same dialect. Of ten families of settlers gathered in any one place, two might well have spoken London English, three or four others one of the southern or southeastern county dialects. There would be in addition a couple of families speaking northern English and another two or three employing a western dialect. In the course of their being in constant contact with each other, compromises for the everyday terms in which their dialects differed would normally have developed, and one could reasonably expect to find a southern English term for a water receptacle, a northern word for earthworm, and a western designation for sour milk. Matters of pronunciation would eventually, perhaps after a slightly longer time, be compromised in much the same manner. Moreover, the resultant compromises for various localities would be different. In the first place, no two localities would have had exactly the same proportions of speakers of the various English dialects, and even if they had, the two localities would not have arrived at precisely the same set of compromises. Thus, early in our history we developed, at various points on the Atlantic seaboard, a number of local cultures, each with distinctive social characteristics of its own—including a dialect which was basically a unique blend of British types of speech, supplemented in its vocabulary by borrowings from the Indians and from Dutch and German neighbors.

With the beginning of the nineteenth century, three changes occurred which were to have a profound effect upon the language situation in America. First, the industrial revolution resulted in the growth of a number of industrial centers, uprooting a considerable proportion of the farm population and concentrating it in the cities. The development of the railroad and other mechanical means of travel increased greatly the mobility of the average person. The large-scale migrations westward also resulted in some resettlement and shifting, even among those who did not set out on the long trek. All of this resulted in a general abandonment of narrowly local speech forms in favor of fewer, more or less general, regional types. Some local speech forms have remained even to the present day. These are usually known as relics, particularly when they are distributed in isolated spots over an area rather than in concentration. *Open stone peach,* for example, is a relic for freestone peach, occurring in Maryland. *Smurring up,* 'getting foggy,' survives as a relic in eastern Maine and more rarely on Cape Cod and Martha's Vineyard.

Even prior to the shifts in population and changes in the culture pattern, certain colonial cities such as Boston, Philadelphia, and Charleston had acquired prestige by developing as centers of trade and foci of immigration. They became socially and culturally outstanding, as well as economically powerful, thus dominating the areas surrounding them. As a consequence, local expressions and pronunciations peculiar to the countryside came to be replaced by new forms of speech emanating from these centers. A fairly recent instance of this is to be found in the New England term *tonic* for soda water, practically co-extensive with the area served by Boston wholesalers. Professor Kurath considers the influence of these centers as second only to the influence of the original settlement in shaping the regional types of speech on the Atlantic seaboard and in determining their geographic boundaries.

Nor was the general process of dialect formation by any means completed with the settlement of the Atlantic seaboard. As the land to the west came to be taken up in successive stages (for example, western New York, Michigan, Wisconsin in the North; southern Ohio, Indiana, and southern Illinois in the Midland area) the same mixtures of speech forms among the settlers were present at first, and the same linguistic compromises had to be worked out. The same processes occurred in the interior South, in Texas, and later on in the Far West. Consequently, the complete linguistic history, particularly with respect to regional forms, of the United States will not be known until all of the facts concerning the present regional distribution of speech forms have been collected, and until these facts have been collated with the settlement history of the various areas and the speech types employed by the settlers at the time they moved in. In its entirety this would necessitate a greater knowledge of the local dialects of seventeenth-century England than we have at present.

Moreover, such environmental factors as topography, climate, and plant and animal life also play their parts in influencing the dialect of an area, just as they did in the general transplanting of the English language to America. The complexity and size of the network of fresh-water streams will affect the distribution and meaning of such terms as *brook, creek, branch,* and *river.* In parts of Ohio and Pennsylvania, for example, the term *creek* is applied to a much larger body of water than in Michigan. It is even more obvious that in those parts of the country where snow is a rarity or does not fall at all, there will be no necessity for a battery of terms to indicate coasting face down on a sled. It is not surprising that those areas of the country where cows can be milked outside, for at least part of the year, will develop a specific term for the place where this is done: witness *milk gap* or *milking gap* current in the Appalachians south of the James River. The wealth of terms for various types of fences throughout the country is again dependent, in part at least, on the material which is available for building them, be it stones, stumps, or wooden rails.

Different types of institutions and practices which developed in various parts of the country also had their effect upon regional vocabulary. Those settlements which did not follow the practice of setting aside a parcel of land for common grazing purposes had little use for such terms as *green* or *common*. The meaning of *town* will vary according to the place and importance of township and county respectively in the organization of local government. The same principle applies equally well to foods of various kinds, which reflect not only materials which are readily available but folk practices as well. The German custom of preparing raised doughnuts as Lenten fare survives in the Pennsylvania term *fossnocks,* shortened from *Fastnachtskuchen.*

Finally, a new invention or development introduced into several parts of the country at the same time will acquire different names in various places. The baby carriage, for example, seems to have been a development of the 1830's and '40's, and this is the term which developed in New England. Within the Philadelphia trade area, however, the article became known as a *baby coach,* whereas *baby buggy* was adopted west of the Alleghenies and *baby cab* in other regions throughout the country. Nor have we necessarily seen an end to this process. Within the last two decades the building of large, double-lane, limited-access automobile highways has been undertaken in various parts of the country, yet the terminology for them differs considerably. In eastern New York, Connecticut, and Rhode Island these are *parkways,* but *turnpikes* in Pennsylvania, New Jersey, New Hampshire, Maine, Massachusetts, Ohio, and Indiana. In New

York *thruway* is used, and they are *expressways* in Michigan and *freeways* in California. These would seem to be regionalisms in the making.

It is of interest also to look at the dialect situation from the point of view of various words which are employed in various parts of the country for the same concept. One of the most interesting and instructive distributions is to be found in connection with the terms used for *earthworm*. This word is used by cultivated speakers in the metropolitan centers. *Angleworm* is the regional term in the North, *fishworm* in the Midland area, and *fishing worm* in the coastal South. *Fish bait* and *bait worm* occupy smaller areas within the extensive *fishworm* region, but are also distributed over a wide territory.

In addition, there is a large number of local terms, many of which are used principally by the older and less-educated inhabitants. The Merrimack Valley, in New Hampshire, and Essex County, Massachusetts, have *mud worm*. *Eace worm* is used in Rhode Island. *Angle dog* appears in upper Connecticut, and *ground worm* on the Eastern Shore of Virginia. *Red worm* is used in the mountains of North Carolina, and an area around Toledo, Ohio, uses *dew worm*. Scattered instances of *rainworm* appear on Buzzards Bay in Massachusetts, throughout the Pennsylvania German area, and in German settlements in North Carolina, Maine, and Wisconsin. We have, thus, a wealth of older local terms, three distinct regional words, and the cultivated *earthworm* appearing in addition as a folk word in South Carolina and along the North Carolina and Virginia coast. Where and how did the various terms originate, and what can be determined about their subsequent history?

Earthworm itself is not an old word; it appears to have been compounded only shortly before the earliest English migrations to America. The earliest *Oxford English Dictionary* citation of the word in its present form is 1591; it appears also as *yearth worm* some thirty years earlier. The various regional terms all seem to have been coined in America; the dictionaries either record no British citations or fail to include the words at all.

The local terms have a varied and interesting history. *Mud worm* seems to occur in standard British English from the beginning of the nineteenth century on. *Eace worm,* as a combined form, goes back at least to Middle English; the first element was a term for 'bait' as early as Aelfric; it is used today in a number of southern counties in England from Kent to Gloucester. *Angle dog* is used currently in Devonshire. *Ground worm,* though coined in England, was transferred to North Carolina and Maryland in the eighteenth century. *Red worm* appears first in England in 1450 and continues through to the mid-nineteenth century, though chiefly in books on fishing, as does *dew worm,* which goes back even farther, to the late Old English period. *Rainworm,* though it appears in Aelfric as *renwyrm,* may be a reformation, even in British English, on the pattern of *Regenwurm* in German, for there is a gap of seven centuries in the citations in the *Oxford English Dictionary* and there is reason to believe that its revival in 1731 was influenced by the German form. Moreover, with but one exception, it has been cited for the United States only in areas settled by Germans.

Thus we have in the standard cultivated term one of relatively recent British formation. Apparently the regional terms were compounded in America, whereas the local terms represent survivals either of dialect usage or anglers' jargon and one loan translation. It is worth noting that the common Old English term, *angle twicce,* surviving as *angle twitch* in Cornwall and Devon, seems not to have found its way to America, and there are, furthermore, such other English formations as *tag worm, marsh worm,* and *garden worm* which have not been recorded in America.

At times, too, changes in meaning seem to have entered into the dialect situation, as is illustrated by the development of the regional terms *skillet* and *spider,* the former current in the Midland and the Virginia Piedmont, the latter in the North and in the Southern tidewater area. *Frying pan* is the urban term and is slowly supplanting the others. *Spider* was originally applied to the cast-iron pan with short legs, from which the name was

presumably derived, but it was ultimately transferred to the
flat-bottomed pan as well. This would seem also to explain the
local term *creeper*, used in Marblehead, Massachusetts. *Skillet*,
a term of doubtful etymology, first appears in English in 1403,
when it was applied to a long-handled brass or copper vessel
used for boiling liquids or stewing meat. It is still so used in
dialects throughout England. The shift in meaning to a frying
pan took place only in America, but an advertisement of 1790,
offering for sale 'bakepans, spiders, skillets,' would suggest that
even as late as this a distinction between the two was recognized.
The examples above have been offered only as a suggestion of
the various language processes which have played a part in the
distribution and meaning of some of our dialect terms. It is quite
obvious that no definitive conclusions about these matters can
be reached until the actual facts of dialect distribution are better
known than they are at present.

Thus far our concern has been only with regional dialects or
speech differences, although we have recognized these as occurring particularly on certain social levels. This raises the question
of the extent to which social dialects occur in American English.
Is there a so-called vulgate which has reasonably uniform characteristics throughout the country, and if so, what is it?

For the most part, the language of the uncultivated will be
recognized in terms of its inflectional characteristics, or at any
rate it is this aspect of the language for which the most authentic
information is available. Before these matters are taken up in
detail, therefore, one or two points about the operation of inflections should be clearly understood.

First, we must recognize that our inflectional endings are in
reality a series of patterns which are applied quite automatically
whenever a situation demanding their use occurs. Even in highly
inflected languages, such as Modern Finnish or Ciceronian Latin,
the speaker does or did not find it necessary to recite a paradigm
to determine the proper case ending. Second, throughout the
history of the language, there are two forces constantly at work
upon the inflectional system: sound change, which often intro-

duces irregularities or disturbances in the system, and analogy, which tends to simplify or to straighten these out by extending the scope of the already existing pattern. As we look at some of the features of present-day substandard English, we shall see how these forces operate.

Possibly the one inflectional form most characteristic of the nouns in substandard American English is the unchanged plural after numbers: *six mile down the road, five foot tall*, and similarly applied to *month, year*, and *gallon*. Actually this is the preservation of an old partitive genitive plural after numbers, which resisted the analogical extension of the *-s* inflection to cases other than the nominative and accusative. The lesson to be learned from this is that the substandard language frequently preserves linguistically older forms than Standard English, a fact not too surprising when it is recalled that substandard English depends entirely on oral transmission from one generation to another.

Certain of the pronoun inflections, however, demonstrate precisely the contrary tendency: the development of innovations or new forms and patterns in substandard English. This is true, for example, of the possessive pronoun in its so-called absolute form, which in the standard language represents a strange and inconsistent mixture of patterns indeed. *Mine* and the archaic *thine* are formed from the adjectival form by adding *-n*. *Hers, ours, yours*, and *theirs*, on the other hand, add *-s* to the adjectival form, probably on the pattern of the noun genitive. *His* and *its* are indistinguishable so far as their secondary and absolute forms are concerned. In contrast, the substandard *mine, yourn, hisn, hern, ourn, theirn* present a perfectly regular pattern formed by an analogical extension of *mine* and *thine* to the third person singular and to the plural forms. At one time or another, several of these forms appeared in Standard English, but they seem never to have caught on and were, as we have seen, replaced in part by the *-s* forms. But the substandard language carried out the innovation completely and consistently except for *its*, which is virtually never used in the absolute form anyway.

A further point worth mentioning is that although speakers of the substandard language are rarely trained in school grammar, their language observes its own laws—not those of Standard English—in a thoroughly rigorous manner. *Hisn,* for example, is the absolute, not the secondary or adjectival form, and the two are never confused. Most speakers of the substandard language might be expected to say *the book is hisn;* no speaker of substandard English would ever say *hisn book.*

The reflexive pronouns give us another instance of a more regular operation of analogy on the substandard level than on the standard. In Standard English, *myself, yourself, ourselves,* and *yourselves* are combinations of the genitive pronoun plus the singular or plural of the *-self* form; *himself* and *themselves* employ the object form of the pronoun, whereas *herself* and *itself* could be either. Substandard English, in substituting *hisself* and *theirself* in the third person and adhering to the singular of *self* in *ourself* and *yourself* (plural), is not only more consistent but more economical in that the latter combinations signal the plural only once and avoid the tautology of the plural *-selves.* The only ambiguity is in the second person, but the second personal pronoun has lost its distinctions between singular and plural anyway, except for the Southern form *you all.*

One curious feature of the substandard pronoun is the substitution of the object for the subjective form in such sentences as *Us girls went home, John and her was married, Me and him was late.* This seems to occur principally when the subject is compound or when one or more words intervene between the pronominal subject and verb, as in *us girls.* Postverbally the reverse type of substitution (subject for object form) is often found, as in *She gave it to mother and I, She took all of we children.* Since these locutions are found considerably higher up the social and educational scale than those previously mentioned, it is possible, at least, that they are the result of overcorrection.

Space does not permit an exhaustive treatment of all the inflectional forms of substandard English, but a few that are typical deserve brief mention. *Them* as a demonstrative adjective (*them books*) probably harks back to the days when the English article and the demonstrative *that* (dative ðǣm) were one and the same form. The multiple negative was also a regular and accepted feature of older English, as was the so-called flat adverb, without the -*ly* derivative suffix. However, since the standard and substandard languages are undoubtedly farthest apart with respect to verb forms, some features of the verbs of the vulgate, as they were once called by the late Robert Menner, should be described.

First of all, with respect to the present tense, there is some tendency to dispose of the distinctive inflection for the third person singular, either by eliminating it in such forms as *he want, she write,* etc., or by extending the peculiar form of the third person to the first and second—*I has some good friends, You is in lots of trouble.*

It is in the preterit and past participle forms, chiefly of those verbs which are somewhat irregular in Standard English, that the widest deviations occur. Again one may recognize here the two opposing tendencies: the retention of older forms and the simplification of irregularities through analogical processes.

The older forms retained in the substandard language owe their origin chiefly to the fact that the so-called strong verb in earlier stages of the language had four principal parts, a past tense singular as well as a past tense plural, in addition to the infinitive and present participle. Thus *writ* as a past tense of *write* represents an older preterit plural form, as do *begun* and *swum.*

On the other hand, the overwhelming tendency in English verb development throughout the last seven or eight centuries has been toward an aggrandizement of the regular or weak inflection at the expense of the older minor conjugations. This is in effect a tendency toward a two-part verb, the infinitive or present stem opposed to an identical past tense and past participle. In general, this has been brought about through analogical processes. Deviant substandard forms are usually the result of analogies which have not operated in Standard English and which take one of two directions: either the extension of the weak past inflections to such irregular verbs as *know* and *see* (*knowed, seed*) or the amalgamation of the strong preterit or past participle with the complementary form (*I taken, he done* as preterits; *have gave, have wrote, has went* as past participial forms).

In one sense, therefore, the differences between the grammatical systems of standard and substandard English represent a difference in the direction and rapidity of inflectional changes. Unquestionably the easy transition from one social class to another in the United States has resulted in a very hazy line of demarcation between what is acceptable and what is considered illiterate. According to the most rigorous schoolbook standard, some of the language employed in American legislative councils and in business life would not pass muster. The awareness of this, combined with an unrealistic treatment of language in our schools, has resulted at times in a defiance of these questionable standards. More often it has given people a guilt complex about the language they use. James West, in his community study entitled *Plainville, U.S.A.* makes a pertinent comment upon this very point:

> 'Inferior' English has been selected as a primary and almost universal trait for apology because the school teacher, the press, and the radio have all cooperated to arouse self-consciousness concerning dialect forms, phrases, and phonetics. All but the 'most backwoodsy' speakers frequently ridicule and parody the stratum or strata of speech beneath or older than their own, and at the same time feel uncertain about their own usages.

Consequently, few Americans, even among the well-educated, are confident and assured of the essential aptness and correctness of their speech. It will take at least a half-century of a more enlightened attitude toward language in the public schools to bring about any perceptible change in this state of affairs. In the meantime, what is sadly needed is an entertaining, yet scientific, treatment of vulgate speech to demonstrate how interesting a phenomenon it really is.

8

The Names Thereof

The moment we move out of our accustomed environment we are assailed by a host of unfamiliar names—names for persons, names for places, and names for things, to echo the well-worn definition of a noun. Most visitors to the nation's capital cannot fail to be aware of the alphabetical designations for a host of streets and the use of the names of the states for avenues. The New England family names on the mail boxes of rural Vermont, the designations for manufactured products typical of a particular area all make their impact upon the visitor. And by extension, the totality of naming practices in America produces a powerful effect upon the newcomer to our shores, just as those of France, Germany, or even England have upon the American traveler. When he reaches England, Stoke Poges, Christmas Common, and Netherstowey convey a flavor quite different from anything he has previously encountered.

It is scarcely necessary to demonstrate in detail that the problem of naming in the United States is vast and complex. The expanse of territory to be supplied with names is huge; the political subdivisions are almost innumerable when one considers the forty-eight states with counties ranging from a dozen or so to more than a hundred for each state, the subdivisions of the counties into townships or towns, the rivers, their tribu-

151

taries, the lakes, the hills and mountains, the prairies and plains, to say nothing of the cities and villages. And of course, there are the people themselves, and here we encounter some quite different naming problems and practices, of which more will be said later. Let us begin with place designations.

In general the place-naming practices reflect those tendencies and influences which operated upon the American vocabulary as a whole. Just as the colonists came to the shores of this country speaking the English language current at the time, so they brought with them a host of names for places familiar to them in their own country, which they immediately applied to their newly created settlements. Particularly in New England do we find perpetuated names common in the English countryside. Bath in Maine, Brentwood and Croydon in New Hampshire, Danby and Maidstone in Vermont, Andover, Leominster, and Salisbury in Massachusetts, Colchester and Norwich in Connecticut, Exeter in Rhode Island are only a few instances, typical of dozens of others.

Even before the arrival of the permanent settlers, the explorers and in part the monarchs who financed and promoted the expeditions exercised some control over the names which were conferred upon vast stretches of unexplored territory and the bodies of water adjacent to them. Many of these names were commemorative. Cape Ann was named in honor of the mother of King Charles. Cape Elizabeth, Cape James, Cape Henry are all self-explanatory, as indeed are Virginia, the Carolinas, Maryland, and Georgia, each of the last-named reflecting a different period of discovery and settlement. Moreover, as settlement spread westward, many of the traditional English names were reapplied to newly established places on the frontier. We know, for example that Boston, Massachusetts, was named for the city in Lincolnshire, but it is more than likely that those in Alabama, Indiana, Kentucky, Missouri, New York, Ohio, Pennsylvania, Tennessee, Texas, and possibly the one in Georgia, derived their name from the already existing Massachusetts settlement.

The kind of name transference that has just been described

strikes one as a highly conscious process compared with the
almost casual way in which place names seem to have developed
in England and Western Europe. Of course there the place
names reflect centuries of historical and cultural development,
to say nothing of changes in languages as well. But nowhere in
the many excellent and detailed investigations into the place
names of Germany, France, and England does one sense the
urgency of naming on a large scale, nor is he likely to encounter
for these countries many specific statements of the reasons why
one or another name was finally—and consciously—agreed upon.
In this connection George R. Stewart, in his fine comprehensive
treatment of American place names, cites two passages which
are very revealing. The first of these, by a Puritan Chronicler,
sets forth the basis of the commemorative practice in these terms:

> Why they called it Dorchester [Massachusetts] I never heard;
> but there was some of Dorsetshire and some of ye town of
> Dorchester that settled there, and it is very likely it might be
> in honor of ye aforesaid Revd. Mr. White of Dorchester.

The second, a Connecticut court resolution of 1658, broadens
this into a general principle:

> Whereas, it hath been a commendable practice of the inhabi-
> tants of all the Colonies of these parts, that as this Country
> hath its denomination from our dear native Country of Eng-
> land, and thence is called New England, so the planters, in
> their first settling of most new plantations have given names
> to those plantations of some Cities and Towns in England,
> thereby intending to keep up and leave to posterity the me-
> morial of several places of note there, as Boston, Hartford,
> Windsor, York, Ipswich, Braintree, Exeter.

Also, the concluding portion of this same resolution points
to a development which was to occur over and over again in
the course of the settlement of the country:

> Considering that there is yet no place in any of the Colonies
> that has been named in memory of the City of London, there

being a new plantation within this Jurisdiction of Connecticut settled upon the fair River of Monhegin, in the Pequot Country, it being an excellent harbor and a fit and convenient place for future trade, it being also the only place which the English of these parts have possessed by conquest, and that by a very just war upon that great and warlike people, the Pequots, that therefore they might thereby leave to posterity the memory of that renowned city of London, from whence we had our transportation, have thought fit, in honor to that famous City, to call the said plantation, New London.

Not only was New London born of this reasoning, but the innumerable combinations with *New* which dot the country from coast to coast. In addition to the ten Bostons in states other than Massachusetts, we must also reckon with eight New Bostons. Four New Baltimores, five New Bedfords, an even dozen New Londons, six New Richmonds serve to give some idea of the prevalence of this combination in a country that for three centuries considered itself new, wholly or in part.

Just as the American vocabulary as a whole added elements of the various non-English cultures which the colonists encountered, so do the place names reflect these same linguistic contacts, often more extensively than the vocabulary as a whole. This is particularly true of the American Indian languages, where the pervasiveness, the extent, and the frequency of their influence upon our place names far exceeds their general effect upon the American lexicon. From one part of the country to another, from Walla Walla to Waxahachie, from Kissimmee to Kalamazoo, our map is dotted with all kinds of Indian names. They are on the lips of our people every day. They constitute an integral part of the flavor of American life and culture. Even the names of twenty-six of the forty-eight states of the Union are Indian in origin.

These place names represent various types of linguistic treatment. Often the English-speaking settlers merely took over, more or less accurately, the name given to a place by the Indians themselves. Frequently such names were descriptive of the landscape or of the life about it. Mackinac Island has already been explained as a shortening of *Michilimackinac*, 'great turtle.' Mississippi is simply 'big river.' The name Chicago has several interpretations, the most likely being 'place of wild onions,' the final -*o*, serving really as a locative suffix. Occasionally Indian names were given to places by white settlers who were familiar with one or another of the various Indian languages. This was the case with Negaunee ('high place') in Michigan, named by Peter White, and a number of Michigan counties have Indian names coined by Henry Rowe Schoolcraft. In fact Schoolcraft, an assiduous collector of Indian lore—Longfellow based his *Hiawatha* upon Schoolcraft's work—let his enthusiasm for Algonquian names run away with him to such a degree that the Michigan legislature finally revolted against such unpronounceable specimens as Kaykakee, Mikenauk, Notipekago, Aishcum, and Cheonoquet, and substituted a number of simple Irish names like Clare, Emmet, and Roscommon for those which the expert had devised.

Many times in the course of our name giving, the Indian name was translated into its English equivalent. As the survey of place names in South Dakota puts it, 'When a creek is called White Thunder, Blue Dog, or American Horse, the Indian influence is obvious, since these adjectives are not those which a white man would use with these nouns. Four Horns, Greasy Horn, and Dog Ear are other examples.' The survey neglected to mention Stinking Water and Stinking Bear creeks, both of which are further convincing and delightful illustrations of this same process. A somewhat more complex, though still typical, history is furnished by the name Yellowstone, an anglicization of the French *roche jaune*, which in turn was probably a translation of the Minnataree name *Mitsiadazi*.

Finally, American Indian tribal or personal names are often applied to places. To quote again from George R. Stewart's *Names on the Land*, 'Famous chiefs were admired as good warriors or defenders of the liberty of their people. Powhatan, Tecumseh, Pontiac . . . became names of towns and counties. Even the grotesque Cornplanter appeared as a Pennsylvania town. Osceola, a Florida Seminole, gave his name to seventeen places in far-scattered states.' Similarly such names as Genesee, Muskingum, Miami, Huron, and Narragansett all perpetuate the names of Indian nations.

In the New York area many place names have remained as a testimony to the original Dutch settlement. Many of these were imported directly from Holland, among which may be included Harlem, Staten (Island), Flushing (Dutch *Vlissingen*), Yonkers, and Spuyten Duyvil. In addition we took from the Dutch a large number of compounding place-name elements such as *-dorp*, *-kill* for 'channel,' *-hook*, *-clove* for 'ravine.' Sometimes these combined with Dutch elements, at other times with English, as can be seen in formations like Sandy Hook, Kinderhook, Peekskill, Catskill, Schuylkill, New Dorp, North Clove, and the tautological formation Clove Valley. Later areas of Dutch settlement appear to have employed only such direct borrowings as Vriesland, Zealand, Drenthe, Overisel, and Graafschap, all in Michigan, and these only for town names. In Michigan and Iowa the Dutch naming influence did not extend to features of the topography.

A well-defined sector of place names in the United States gives evidence of the originally French colonial status of a considerable portion of the country. These names fall into two broad classes: such descriptive terms as Detroit, Au Sable, Ecorse, Grand Blanc, Eau Claire, Prairie du Chien, Fond du Lac, and commemorative names like Louisiana, La Salle, Charlevoix, Marquette, Lafayette, St. Ignace, and St. Joseph. The descriptive terms were often given by the French themselves, or at times were actually translations of earlier Indian place names, as for example Baton Rouge, a translation of Choctaw *istrouma* 'red post,' and Platte River (originally Rivière Plate), an attempt to render *ni*, 'river' and *bthaska*, 'spreading flatness.'

Two other place-naming practices stemming from French influence should be mentioned. Hundreds of towns and cities all over the United States have the French suffix *-ville* as a part of their name (Nashville, Louisville, Jacksonville, etc.) a feature which is certainly not common in England. The *-ville* craze, resulting at times in such bizarre formations as Applebachsville, appears to have begun late in the eighteenth century and to have attained startling proportions early in the nineteenth. Matthew Arnold's comment on this practice is worth quoting: 'What people in whom the sense of beauty and fitness was quick could have invented or could tolerate the hideous names ending in *ville,* the Briggsvilles, Higginsvilles, Jacksonvilles, rife from Maine to Florida; the jumble of unnatural and inappropriate names everywhere?'

Less obvious but of equal importance is the word order in such names as Lake Superior and Lake Champlain, where the general or common noun comes first and is followed, as in French, by the modifying or specific term. All the names of the Great Lakes follow this syntactical pattern, retaining their original order.

Place names of Spanish origin are centered chiefly in Florida and the Southwest. Their number has been estimated at approximately 2000. At least a fifth of those in California are saints' names—witness San Diego, Santa Monica, Santa Barbara, San Francisco—commemorating either the patron saint of the explorer who named the spot or the particular saint's day on which the discovery was made.

Some of the original Spanish names have since been translated: Rio de los Santos Reyes has been displaced by the much more prosaic Kings River, and Rio de las Plumas by Feather River. In addition there may be found such hybrid combinations as Hermosa Beach and Point Loma, some of which, like the first, at least make sense, and others, like the second, betray the linguistic naïveté of the realtor who developed the subdivision and gave it its name.

One well-defined layer in the lexicon of American place names assumes far more prominence than in the vocabulary generally. These are names associated with classical antiquity. In a sense the tradition may be said to have begun with William Penn, who after his original suggestion of New Wales as a name for the land he was about to acquire in America was rejected by the

King's secretary, proposed Sylvania as a second choice. The outcome, Pennsylvania, was placed in the charter by Charles II. Likewise the principal city of the new colony derived its name from classical sources, and almost every schoolboy in America knows that Philadelphia means 'city of brotherly love.'

A second impetus toward the adoption of Greek and Latin names came from a series of events occurring in the state of New York soon after the country gained its independence. First, a town meeting at Vanderheyden's Ferry in 1789 decided to rename that settlement Troy. Just a year later the Military Tract in the Finger Lakes area was divided into twenty-five townships; the commission entrusted with the disposal of public lands gave to all but three of these the name of a person celebrated in classical antiquity, ranging from Hector, Ulysses, and Romulus to Brutus and Cato, including also the poets Virgil and Ovid. The original inspiration seems to have dried up at the end, permitting the inclusion of Locke, Milton, and Dryden, although these by no means detracted from the prevailing learned atmosphere. From these beginnnings it was but a step to the establishment of a whole series of classical city names: again in New York we find a Carthage as well as a Rome, an Ithaca, a Corinth, and a Syracuse, and an Ilion in addition to a Troy.

As the New York settlers went on to the west, many of the classical names were transferred. The Ithacas in Michigan and Wisconsin, the Troys in Wisconsin and Iowa can undoubtedly be explained on this basis, but actually something more than population movement and name transference is involved here. There was an awakening of interest in Greek and Roman antiquity throughout the country. Part of this can be explained by the development of secondary education; in dozens of academies the classical course, with Latin and Greek language, literature, history, and geography for its subject matter, was the accepted preparatory curriculum for college work. Also, as a consequence of our break from English political tradition, we tended in our first flush of republican enthusiasm to look to Rome as a model. Even architecturally the classical revival was sweeping the country, beginning first in the east but extending virtually to the Mississippi by the 1840's and 1850's, dotting the new towns and cities with courthouses built like Doric temples, homes with columned porticos, college buildings reproducing the detail of the Parthenon. The eleven Romes, the nine Corinths, the twelve Spartas, the two Spartanburgs and the lone Spartansburg in the United States are indicative of but one aspect of a general cultural movement, which found a further outlet in the extension of -*sylvania* and -*opolis* as place-naming elements.

Another important layer of place names in America consists of those drawn from the Bible. With the impulse for religious groups to emigrate as organized bodies seeking freedom of worship so widespread from the very beginning of American colonization almost to the very end, it would have been strange indeed if the Bible had not been employed for this purpose. Here it is interesting to observe that of the New England colonies, it is Connecticut rather than Massachusetts, despite the customary association of the latter with Puritanism, which has a well-defined sector of Biblical place names: Bethel, Bethlehem, Canaan, Gilead, Goshen, Hebron, Jordan, Lebanon, Mt. Carmel, and Sharon. Stewart has suggested that these arose from the religious fervor accompanying the Great Awakening rather than from the earliest period of settlement.

The Moravians and other minor sects from Middle Europe which came to settle in Pennsylvania, spread into New York and later moved southward as far as North Carolina and westward to Indiana and Iowa were also responsible for a good many of the Bethels, Bethlehems, and Goshens, as well as Emmaus, Ephrata, and Nazareth. The Latter-day Saints left their mark upon the map of Utah with names like Moroni, Nephi, Lehi, and Alma, drawn from the Book of Mormon, and also with Zion, Moab, Paradise, and Eden from the Bible itself. In fact they almost succeeded in naming the state Deseret, a term for honey bee, also drawn from the Book of Mormon.

Nothing short of a volume could even begin to do justice to all the naming practices which came to be employed; space per-

mits the mention of only one or two others. From the time of
Roger Williams on, there was always a marked strain of Utopian-
ism prominent in the settlement of America. Groups motivated
by ideologies ranging all the way from socialism to vegetarianism
(and sometimes including both) came from abroad or collected
in this country, determined to establish new social orders. Not
infrequently the ideals or aspirations of these groups were reflected by the names which they bestowed upon their newly
founded communities. Thus there appear among our place names
such abstractions as Providence, Concord, Hope, and Harmony.
Another facet of this same naming practice is much more closely
connected with the normal political development of the country
and our early struggles for national existence. Places called
Liberty, Union, Freedom, and Independence dot the length and
breadth of the land, either in their simple forms or in such combinations as Uniontown and Libertyville.

How a single name can give rise to a brood of others is particularly well illustrated by an occurrence in southern Illinois.
When settlers came to establish a new village at the junction of
the Ohio and the Mississippi rivers, the general topography of
the area suggested the site of the capital of Egypt; accordingly
it was called Cairo. As other villages came into being, the pattern was extended, and we find Karnak, Thebes, and Joppa.
Finally the whole area became known as Egypt, a name which
has persisted well over a century though it is recorded on no
map. For a time there was even a distinction between Little
Egypt, the territory immediately surrounding Cairo, and Greater
Egypt, applied to a somewhat more extended area. Unfortunately, since Little Egypt was also the sobriquet of the notorious hip-wriggler of the first Chicago World's Fair, its popularity
as a place designation diminished somewhat understandably,
and now only Greater Egypt remains in use.

Thus far our principal concern has been the importation of
place names. Nevertheless all the other linguistic processes which
contributed to the development of the American vocabulary as
a whole are reflected in our place-naming practices, very often

in connection with the common nouns, the toponymic designations which enter into place-name combinations. For example, the American as well as the general English colonial use of *creek* reflects a change of meaning from 'inlet' to 'stream tributary.' The *Oxford English Dictionary* in its treatment of this word offers a very cogent account of the circumstances responsible for this change:

> Probably the name was originally given by the explorers of a river to the various inlets or arms observed to run out of it, and of which only the mouths were seen in passing; when at a later period these 'creeks' were explored, they were often found to be tributaries of great length; but they retained the designation originally given, and 'creek' thus received an application entirely unknown in Great Britain.

Today *creek* is probably the most common American term for something smaller than a river, often tributary to it, but its application in various parts of the country depends in part at least upon the nature, size, and extent of the network of waterways. Many a creek in Ohio would be called a river in the neighboring state of Michigan. *Creek* has entered into hundreds if not thousands of place-name combinations throughout the country.

Instances of transference from British regional or dialect use are to be found in *run,* also a term for a small stream, and *swamp,* the common American designation for marshy or boggy land. The former appears to have been originally Scottish or northern English; even its first citation in the literary language is to be found in the works of Boswell. This is more than a century later than its appearance in America, where it was used by early settlers and explorers in Massachusetts and Virginia. *Swamp* is recorded late in the seventeenth century as a south and east country word, and *sump* with this meaning is to be found in the north. In America the earliest recorded examples of the term occur with reference to Virginia, but it spread very rapidly to all parts of the eastern coast.

Gulch, chiefly a western American term for a ravine, canyon, or gully, also has its origins in the English dialect vocabulary, but this time with functional change; its probable origin was a verb *gulch* or *gulsh*, 'to sink in.' *Bluff* for a steep river bank or shore is likewise the product of a transference of grammatical function. It was used first as an adjective, applied originally to ships that presented a broad flattened front and then to a shore or coastline of the same general contour, especially in the combinations *bluff land* and *bluff point*. Finally in South Carolina and Georgia the nouns were simply omitted, the adjective thus acquiring substantive use.

In short, toponymy is one of the divisions of the lexicon where sharp differences have developed between American and British English. Words like *fen, heath, moor,* and *coomb,* to mention only a few, common in England, invariably have a literary flavor for the American because he encounters them only in books. They are not a part of his everyday vocabulary. The topography of America was just different enough from that of the mother country to favor the development of an indigenous set of toponyms, which in turn occur over and over again in our place names.

Word blending too has had a very specific role in the development of our place names, particularly in connection with cities and villages situated athwart our state borders and to a lesser extent our national boundaries. Texarkana is probably the best known of these, but there are also Kenova (Kentucky, Ohio, West Virginia), Calneva, Calvada, Calada, Calzona, Calexico, and Delmarva (Delaware, Maryland, Virginia). According to Stewart, some sixty names of this type mark the lines between various Southern and Far Western states. Upon occasion the blending process in place names operates in a somewhat more cryptic fashion. Marenisco, Michigan, was formed from the first syllables of the names of the first woman settler, Mary Relief Niles Scott, and according to one story at least Azusa, California, grows everything from A to Z in the USA.

Thus far our discussion has been confined to the names of cities, villages, and features of the landscape. Some mention must be made as well of American street-naming practices, and in this connection the pattern of growth or development of the American cities is important. They did not grow by gradual extension or accretion as did their European counterparts; usually they were laid out or plotted in advance of settlement. At the very least this necessitated the naming of many streets at a single time, permitting a process of free association to operate. More often street names were given on the basis of some ordered scheme.

This was true even as early as the seventeenth century when Philadelphia was plotted. The streets running in one direction were simply numbered; those cutting them at right angles were named—or at least many of them—after the various trees which grew there. In so doing Penn originated a system the essential elements of which were to be followed in city after city in the new continent. These elements are, first of all, a four-square or rectangular plan, with streets running at right angles to each other; second, the frequent use of numbers for the one tier or series of streets, often reaching into the hundreds, as in present-day New York and Chicago; third, a varied but nonetheless systematic scheme for naming the second series of streets. The use of the letters of the alphabet in Washington, D.C., has already been mentioned. Often a row of streets will be named after the Presidents of the United States in order; many a city has at least the vestigial remnants of such a system, with Washington Street somewhere near the center of business, followed by Adams, Jefferson, and so on, the name of the last president in the series indicating just about the time that portion of the city was platted. In one section of Denver, Colorado, the streets were given Indian tribal names arranged in alphabetical order, from Acoma and Bannock to Yuma and Zuni. A second series honored famous Americans, also in alphabetical order beginning with Alcott and Bryant; a third perpetuates the names of United States senators, a fourth the justices of the Supreme Court. Whatever scheme or system is followed is irrelevant; the point is that a system exists. Still another kind of schematization is to be found

in the distinction between the term *street* for thoroughfares running in one direction and *avenue* for those at right angles to
them, the plan followed in the portion of Manhattan which was
plotted early in the nineteenth century.

We must remember, too, that this is a continuing process; as
new subdivisions are added to cities, the problem must be faced
again and again. Any collection of names may be drawn on for
the purpose. One portion of Los Angeles is heavily indebted to
the novels of Sir Walter Scott. State capitals sometimes use the
names of the counties in that state, a practice suggested by the
application of state names to the diagonal avenues in Washington, D.C.

There is also Main Street, that most typically American designation for the principal thoroughfare, which attained such
prominence as the title of a popular and important novel that in
many ways it has become a symbol of small-town life. In England the principal street is often called High, the adjective
denoting importance rather than elevation, just as it is used there
in *high road* and *highway*. There are some High Streets in the
older cities along the eastern seaboard of the United States, but
apparently as settlement moved inward into hillier country, *high*
came to suggest physical elevation. Consequently the principal
street in a village was spoken of as 'the main street,' and eventually this became petrified into a proper name. As early as 1687
a Pennsylvania record was entitled, 'A late Order for ye Viewing
and Discussing a maine Road from ye Center of Phildelphia ye
Shortest way to ye falls.' Most American cities bordering or
spanning a river have a Front Street; a Market Street is to be
found in many business sections.

Another feature of American street naming is the variety of
substitute terms for the word *street*. The use of *avenue* has
already been mentioned. According to Stewart:

> The French *avenue*, meaning usually the tree-bordered ap-
> proach to a country-house, had been used in English for some
> time. It had even attained rhetorical usage, as when a Revo-
> lutionary orator cried out: 'Oppression stalked at noon-day

through every avenue of your cities!' But let oppression stalk
where it might, no American had Avenue as his address until
the founding of Washington. Even the later popularity of
Avenue may be partially credited to New York.

Court, which in England usually refers to a confined yard or
more or less quadrangular space opening off a street and built
around with houses, is frequently used in the United States for a
short street, not more than one or two blocks or squares in
length. *Boulevard,* scarcely used in England at all, is applied in
America to an exceptionally broad street or main traffic artery
(e.g. Wilshire Boulevard in Los Angeles), and in some parts of
the country refers specifically to streets which reserve a strip at
the center for shade trees. Recently American city planners have
tended to give up the four-square plan for residential districts,
particularly those designed for larger dwellings, in favor of wind-
ing and even circular streets, thus affording variety of contour
and often more lawn space. As a result a number of new names
have come into use, among them *drive, crescent, circle,* and *park-
way. Road* is also employed, presumably for its suggestion of the
suburban. It is thus becoming a mark of distinction in some
quarters to live on something other than a street or avenue.

There are, however, certain street-naming practices current in
some parts of the world which have not established a foothold
in the United States. Except for using the names of our chief
executives and lawmakers on both the state and national level
and an occasional name like Constitution Avenue, we have kept
politics pretty well out of our street names. A Paseo de la Re-
forma is quite unthinkable; we have no Boulevards of the Declaration of Independence or Avenues of the Emancipation Proc-
lamation. Nor do we memorialize the days or dates important in
our national history by attaching them to streets, as is so often
done with the Fifth of May and the Sixteenth of September in
Mexico. And certainly there is a foreign and artificial ring to
Avenue of the Americas, the new name given to Sixth Avenue
in New York.

Moreover, our street names have the quality of permanence;

when they are changed, it is principally to avoid possible confusion arising from similarity or duplication. We seldom rename principal streets after the heroes of the moment, and since our political life is stable, there are no instances here of a rapid succession of names like Kaiser Wilhelm Platz, Friederich Ebert Platz, Adolf Hitler Platz, and Roosevelt Platz, all applied to a single square within a space of thirty years not in one but in many a German city.

For a country of more than 160 million inhabitants whose ancestors came from all parts of the world, a systematic treatment of the personal names would be even more complex than one dealing with place names or with the vocabulary in general. All that can be done here is to mention some of the principal tendencies and attitudes which prevail today.

First, some brief observations about given names are in order. Despite the strong Puritan influence in the northern colonies, the most absurd excesses of Puritan naming practices are somewhat less apparent in New England than in the mother country. True enough, names like Increase and Preserved are to be found among our early settlers, but one rarely encounters such monstrosities as Search-the-Scriptures or Hate-Evil. However, their other practice, that of adopting Old Testament names, often those which were harsh and unpleasant, persisted well into the nineteenth century. Today the Abimelechs, Eliphalets, Zachariahs, and Hezekiahs have virtually disappeared. This is due in part, possibly, to our increasing concern with child psychology and our consequent unwillingness to foist upon our defenseless infants names which they are likely to despise the rest of their days.

As far as the surnames are concerned, the principal force which has affected them is the pressure for conformity, the dislike on the part of most immigrants, and certainly their children, of any trace of their non-English heritage. This is not to say, of course, that foreign surnames do not persist in America. They do, and to a surprising degree. The country was not very old before it had a Van Buren as a president, and any list of names drawn at random today—a sampling of *Who's Who*, the members of Congress, an army promotion calendar—will show a wider diversity of national origin than one is likely to encounter almost anywhere in the world. However, there are often as many concealed or converted foreign names as those which are obviously and openly so.

To begin with, there are names which have been respelled, either out of deference to general English orthographic practice or because our alphabet lacks the necessary characters and diacritics. We have no wedges for *c*'s and *s*'s; thus a Slavic Jakša often becomes Jackson. The lack of the umlaut sign converts a German Müller either into Miller or Muller, with Mueller as an outside possibility. König becomes either Konig or Koenig, or is translated into King.

Since surnames in many languages represent a patronymic compound (son of someone or other) spelled solidly, they are likely to be long and awkward-looking. In American practice these are often clipped, so that Tomaszewski becomes Thomas, Szymanowski is changed into Simon, and Pappadimitricoupoulos emerges as Pappas. Upon occasion such a patronymic as Ivanovich is simply translated into its English equivalent, Johnson.

The longer a national group has been in the country, the greater the process of assimilation to English pronunciation patterns. Thus French Langlois is scarcely to be recognized in Langley, St. Cyr in Sears, or German Huber in Hoover. Snyder is in a sense a respelling of Schneider, but it also demonstrates the lack of an initial *sh-n* cluster in English. Sounds which do not occur in English at all are either approximated or reconstituted, sometimes in ways which on the surface appear to be quite inexplicable. German Bach is often pronounced with the vowel of *law* and no final consonant at all and may be respelled as Baugh.

In addition to respelling and phonetic approximation, translation provides the other principal means of assimilating foreign names. As early as the eighteenth century there is evidence of German Zimmermann, Jäger, Braunfeld, and Grünbaum appear-

ing as Carpenter, Hunter, Brownfield, and Greentree. The process
has continued with other national or linguistic groups—witness
the large numbers of persons of Finnish extraction named Lake
and Hill, translations of Järvinen and Maki, possibly the two
most common Finnish surnames.

Another phenomenon connected with American personal names
is the rise in status of some which in England are regarded as
distinctly lower or lower-middle class. On this subject, Matthew
Arnold once spoke of 'the touch of grossness in our race . . . an
original shortcoming in the more delicate spiritual perceptions,
shown by the natural growth amongst us of such hideous names,
Higginbottom, Stiggins, Bugg! In Ionia and Attica they were
luckier in this respect than "the best race in the world"; by the
Illisus there was no Wragg, poor thing!' It is doubtful that many
Americans would make this association or have this reaction.
For one thing, too many Wraggs and Higginbottoms have become successful; some of them are or have been in *Who's Who*.
Moreover, so much greater an onus has attached itself to some
types of non-English names that Arnold's Wragg would probably
seem first-family or early-settler by comparison. Actually the
only unfavorable reaction to English names at all common in
this country is the association of such given names as Percival,
Reginald, and Archibald with a caricature of upper-class British
traits—effeminacy, the haw-haw Oxford speech, lack of a sense of
humor, in short, the effete and befuddled aristocrat.

Still, not all foreign names have suffered a status loss. Dutch
names, particularly those associated with the Hudson Valley
and old New York, have acquired not merely general acceptance
but indeed an aura of respectability, even of aristocracy. The
same is true of French and Spanish names in those parts of the
country where those nationalities were among the earliest settlers, but here the value system extends only to the surnames. A
young scion of an old and prosperous Knickerbocker family
would not want to be called Klaus or Gerrit; the latter he would
quickly alter to Jerry.

Many special naming problems are so complex that they can

only be mentioned. There are the American Negroes, who after Emancipation had to provide themselves or be provided with permanent surnames, and groups of whom are given to the use of somewhat exotic given names. Even here the practices of the Sea Islands are not those of Harlem. There are the Far Easterners, the Chinese, Japanese, and Hawaiians, with language patterns so completely different from English. There are the Jews, many of whom were originally committed to patriarchal given names combined with a Teutonically compounded surname, but who have recently been subjected to the conflicting tendencies of conformity to native English naming patterns and a revival of interest and pride in pure Hebrew as a replacement for Yiddish. Indeed, a competent study of personal naming in the United States would have as its first requisite a detailed understanding of the complex psychology, the ambitions, hopes, and aspirations as well as the taboos of each of the immigrant groups, ranging from William Bradford to the last Hungarian.

9

The Future of English

The analysis of the development of American English, which has been the concern of the foregoing chapters, has attempted to show the relationship of this development to the most salient features in the cultural life and history of the American people. It would be equally interesting for someone to make a complementary study of the particular facets of British English, and indeed of the English spoken in the various dominions of the Empire, indicating the relationships between language and culture which exist there as well.

But when all is said and done, English, despite the vast numbers who speak it and its widespread dissemination over the globe, is still but a single language, and to paraphrase an earlier commentator, the differences between its widest extremes, though extensive in certain features of the language, are still remarkably few. As a language it is highly unified; more so than many tongues spoken by a far smaller number of people.

This raises the question of the probable future of English. We have already noted that 230 million speakers of English as a first language are spread over four continents. We have noted too that this represents more than a fortyfold, almost a fiftyfold, increase over the number of speakers who used the language in 1600. At that time it was fifth among the languages of the Western world, surpassed in numbers by speakers of French, German,

Spanish, and Italian. In 1750 it was still fifth, Russian having replaced Italian as a fourth. A century later English had gone ahead of the others, the sudden addition of twenty-three million speakers of the language in the United States apparently sufficing to put it into first place.

With this as a background, it might be argued that if the fifty-fold multiplication of the last four centuries were to be cut to merely a fivefold increase over the next four, we might expect one billion speakers of English by 2350—nearly one-half of the present world population. Or the recent rate of increase of from fifteen to twenty million per decade would give us very nearly the same result. The probability of such an increment may be questioned on the ground that the nineteenth-century aggrandizement of English was largely dependent upon the opening up of the North American continent to settlers who eventually adopted the language. With the twentieth century more than half over, it does not seem likely that any single English-speaking country will repeat the feat of the United States in the nineteenth century. Yet Australia, South Africa, and Canada will unquestionably show pronounced gains, and a total of 300 million speakers of English as a first language some time in the twenty-first century is by no means inconceivable. It could reach 350 million. At any rate no other European language, not even Russian, is currently in a position to compete with it.

It is, however, in its development as a second language that the real opportunities for the future development of English seem to lie. It is probably fair to say that after some tinkering with international languages, we can only conclude that no one of them has yet been sufficiently successful to justify much confidence in its future. Consequently, if we are to look forward to any single language which might serve as an international auxiliary—and the increase in rapidity and extent of travel and communication somehow leads us to expect this—such a language will undoubtedly be one of those in use at the present time. The English language would seem to be the best candidate for a number of reasons.

In the first place it is the native language of *two* of the most powerful and influential nations of the world. This is not true of French, German, Russian, Spanish, or Chinese. Moreover, it is used today both in speech and in writing to an extent unsurpassed by any other. It has been estimated that three-fifths of the world's radio stations broadcast in English and that three-fourths of the world's mail is written in the language.

There are in particular certain features of English which make for its convenience as an international auxiliary. Its vocabulary is composed of vast numbers of words both of Teutonic and of Latin origin, making large portions of its word stock readily comprehensible to millions of speakers of other languages. The words are short; the language is free from a complicated inflectional system, giving at least the illusion of ease of mastery. At the same time we must not fail to observe that our wretched spelling system, which so successfully obscures any consistent relationship between the spoken and written forms of the language, will undoubtedly act as a deterrent to some degree, but probably not enough to counterbalance the other factors which have been cited.

It is extremely difficult to estimate the number of speakers of English as a second language: some authorities place the number at fifty million, others at 125 million. Whatever the facts may be, there can be no doubt that it is on the increase. It is replacing French as a second language in the schools of Latin America and in some of the European countries. It has always been important as an auxiliary language in Holland and the Scandinavian countries. Until very recently Russia placed considerable emphasis upon the teaching of English in her schools. Various types of pidgin English serve as a trade language in the Far East. If, within the next century, a more highly interdependent world will have to depend upon bilingualism to conduct its affairs, a doubling of the numbers who now speak English as a second language is not inconceivable. At the end of that time we may assume that probably 500 million people will be speaking some form of English, either as a first or a second language.

This leads to a further question—what kind of English will these half a billion speakers use? What will the language be like? In attempting to answer this, we must remember that English has never been anything like a uniform language. No academy has ever attempted to rule upon its vocabulary and grammar. In America, at least, this lack of uniformity has been due in part to a constant increase in the number of speakers. If the increase should continue at anything like its present rate, it is not likely that a greater uniformity will be established, despite the leveling influence of improved means of communication. This may not be a bad thing; undoubtedly the English language owes much of its vigor to the variety existing within it.

We have seen that a language may be considered from the point of view of its words, its sounds, its inflectional endings, and its patterns of word order. We know also that for the last several centuries the vocabulary of English has been very large, that some words have been borrowed from languages in almost every part of the world. Certain languages, principally Latin, French, and the Scandinavian tongues, have contributed heavily to our present lexicon. Moreover, the dictionaries of the English language at various periods of its history seem to reflect a consistent growth in vocabulary. Dictionaries of Old English, of the language as it was used approximately 1000 years ago, contain about 37,000 words. A fairly complete dictionary of Middle English—that is, of the language of 500 years ago—would have between 50,000 and 70,000 entries. It is likely that a dictionary of Early Modern English, the period of Shakespeare and his contemporaries, would contain at least 140,000 words, and it is a well-known fact that unabridged dictionaries of present-day English have approximately half a million entries.

Even if we consider the probability that the early records of our language are so fragmentary that the numbers just cited for Old and Middle English fall far short of what the language actu-

ally contained, yet the apparent quadrupling of our stock of
words during the last three and a half centuries is significant
evidence of a strong tendency toward vocabulary increase. There
is no reason to suppose that this will not continue.

We have noticed, in addition, that the recent extensions of our
vocabulary have come not so much through word borrowing as
from the manipulation of elements which are already in the language. Such processes as compounding, the addition of derivative
prefixes and suffixes, and change in grammatical function account for considerably more than half of our new words today.
Without question we shall continue to borrow some words from
foreign languages in the future. We did so during both world
wars, and as the language spreads over areas of the Far East,
for example, it is reasonable to look forward to new words coming from Malay, as well as from Russian, possibly even from
Swahili and Bantu, but the principal growth in the English
vocabulary will undoubtedly come as the result of the processes
which have just been mentioned—up to what point is hard to
guess. A doubling of the vocabulary in the next two centuries is
not difficult to conceive in the light of what has happened since
1600.

If the area over which English is spoken and the number of
speakers of English increase, as we expect them to, it is highly
probable that a considerable number of words will be used in
one regional form of English but not in another. It is likely, too,
that the increasing complexities of modern life and modern technology will demand a larger vocabulary of the individual, as has
been evidenced by the replacement of the horse by the automobile, of the town crier by the newspaper, of the candle by
electric lighting. But there has always been a large gap between
the vocabulary of the individual and the total word count of the
language, and this will very likely increase as time goes on.

We may ask next, 'How will the English of the future sound?'
To most of us the language of Chaucer sounds somewhat more
like the present-day speech of one of the Low Countries than
like Modern English, and the early pages of this volume demon-

strate clearly enough that Shakespeare's lines, uttered as we think he and his contemporaries pronounced them, ring somewhat strangely in our ears. Will the speech of our descendants 300 years hence sound equally strange? Or has the English language attained a phonetic stability? There is really no reason to believe that it has. Present differences in the way in which English is pronounced throughout the world may, and in fact do reflect certain differences in the rate at which sound changes have operated in the past.

We shall probably make more progress in attempting to answer this question if we consider it in the light of the various kinds of sounds: consonants, long and short vowels. On the whole our consonants have changed relatively little since the period from the twelfth to the fourteenth centuries, when such pairs as *s* and *z*, *f* and *v* became meaningfully distinct instead of mere variants of the same sound. Prior to that time such contrasts as those of *feel* and *veal* or *ice* and *eyes* could not have occurred in English. It was just about the same time that the *ng* as in *sing* and *long* emerged as a sound in its own right. Since that time English has acquired but one new consonant, the *zh* sound of *vision* or *measure*. Other changes have been confined either to individual words or at most to particular phonetic situations: the development of the *sh* sound in *sugar* and of *j* in *soldier*. There may be more changes of this nature ahead of us, but any basic alteration of the whole consonant system would be surprising.

At the other extreme, the popularly called 'long' vowels have always changed considerably, particularly within the last 500 years. At the beginning of the Christian era, the stressed vowel of the word *home* was pronounced with the sound of *i*, as it still is in the cognate German word *Heim*. By the time of King Alfred the vowel in this word had acquired the sound of *ah*, which then developed to *aw* at approximately 1200. The word attained its present *o*-like quality probably by 1500, as did most others with the same stressed vowel sound. Nor is this a rare or exceptional instance. In the 200 years separating the period of Chaucer from that of Shakespeare, virtually every long vowel in English underwent some sort of change, not only in its own quality but very often in respect to its relationship to other vowel sounds in the language. It is only since the time of Shakespeare, or slightly before, that words such as *read* and *reed, caught* and *bought, pain* and *pane* have come to be pronounced with the same vowel sound, and conversely words such as *coat* and *cot* or *made* and *mad,* then having the same quality of sound, have become differentiated.

Despite the extent and variety of this change, much of it does fit into a pattern. What seems to be involved here is a gradual raising of the tongue and jaw position for making the sounds in question until they reach a point where they cannot be raised any more, after which they develop into diphthongs. Thus the word which Chaucer and his contemporaries pronounced as *moos* is now given the diphthongal pronunciation *mouse*. Conversely, most diphthongs in the earlier periods of the language are now simple vowels—*law* was pronounced earlier with an *ow* sound; today, despite its spelling, it has but a single vowel. Developments as striking as these may easily continue. In fact we may have the beginnings of something like it in the *eh-oo* one encounters in the British pronunciation of words like *know* and *home.*

In comparison, the so-called 'short' vowels have changed very little in the course of the last 1000 years. Words like *bed, this, ox,* and *full* have been pronounced with the same vowels for the last ten centuries and even more. It would seem reasonable, then, to conclude that they will undergo no major changes in the immediate future.

Another kind of pronunciation change is confined particularly to foreign words taken into the language: a shift of stress or accent toward the front. This is occurring today with such words as *cigarette, Detroit, inquiry,* and *robust,* all of which are heard from time to time with the stress on the first syllable. This happened centuries ago to words like *liquor, pleasant,* and *nation,* originally pronounced with principal stress on the final syllable.

From one point of view, the disappearance of secondary stress in the British pronunciation of words like *secretary* and *circumstance* could be considered as a part of the same general development. Without question this tendency will continue to operate, although it is impossible to know which particular words will be affected.

The comparative freedom of English from inflectional or grammatical endings—at least as compared with Latin or German—has often been considered one of its strongest claims as a potential international language. What has happened is that through the years certain other devices have come to take the place of inflections. First, though, let us look at those inflectional suffixes which are indispensable to the structure and operation of English today. The two most important of these are the *-s* plural of nouns and the *-ed* which forms the past tense and past participle of the vast majority of English verbs.

The first of these, originally only one of eight or nine ways of indicating the plural, has expanded to a point where today there are relatively few native nouns which form their plural in any way other than the addition of *-s*. A small number of foreign words, such as *antenna, nucleus,* and *phenomenon,* at times retain the plural inflection of their language of origin. It is possible that the *-s* plural will be extended to some of these, particularly when they pass, as *antenna* has already done, from the learned into everyday language.

In much the same manner the regular *-ed* verb inflection has encroached upon all others during the last ten centuries. Verbs newly admitted into the language have adopted this inflection. Such old verbs as *help* and *climb* have lost their irregular past forms *holp* and *clomb,* which have been replaced in the standard language by *helped* and *climbed.* Even now the very uncertainty which many speakers and writers feel with respect to *strive* and *wake* indicates that a change is under way. The 360 verbs in Old English which indicated changes in tense through alterations of their principal vowel (e.g. *sing, sang, sung*) have been reduced to a mere sixty. The language as a whole now has only about 125 irregular verbs of any kind. It seems safe to predict that this number will become smaller as time goes on.

A few other inflections are now in the process of being replaced by constructions involving what are often called function words. For example, the inflected genitive, or possessive, often alternates with a construction employing the preposition *of: the horse's head, the head of the horse.* Throughout the last several centuries the sphere of *of* has been steadily increasing at the expense of the inflectional ending. We can no longer say *water's glass* for *glass of water,* or *ours one* for *one of ours.* We may well ask whether in time it will seem equally awkward to say *year's vacation, world's fair,* or *St. Joseph's Hospital.* Likewise, the comparative and superlative adjective endings *-er* and *-est* have slowly given way to constructions with *more* and *most.* We are no longer able to employ such formations as *interestinger* and *honestest.* Could this taboo ultimately extend to *prettier* and *hottest?* Finally, it would not seem unreasonable to expect that the few situations where the inflected subjunctive of the verb still remains intact will eventually give way to formations with such auxiliaries as *may, might,* and *should.*

There are also situations in English where the few remaining forms specifically indicative of case, *e.g. me, who, him,* conflict with the normal word-order patterns of the language. In general, an object form such as *me* will follow the verb, whereas a subject form such as *who* will precede it. This tendency toward the fixation of word order accounts for such apparent solecisms as *It is me, Who are you looking for?* Even more important is the general principle behind such developments. When the choice of a form based upon word order conflicts with the choice of a form based upon an inflectional paradigm or pattern, word order generally turns out to be the determining factor. No matter how we feel about these particular constructions, they are undoubtedly here to stay, but because of the scarcity of case-distinctive forms, it is not likely that many more changes of this type will occur.

Word order is, however, one aspect of the larger problem of syntax. In general, largely to compensate for the loss of inflectional endings, English word order has become more rigid. Shakespeare had more freedom than we have now. Will our great-grandchildren have less?

For example, when the modifying elements of place, manner, and time are all included within a single sentence, we are able to say:

> *He wrote the exercise carefully at home this afternoon.*
> *This afternoon he wrote the exercise carefully at home.*
> *He carefully wrote the exercise at home this afternoon.*

Certainly the following constructions seem somewhat more awkward and would occur less frequently:

> *He wrote the exercise at home carefully this afternoon.*
> *He wrote the exercise carefully this afternoon at home.*

We would be even less likely to say:

> *He wrote the exercise at home this afternoon carefully.*
> *He wrote the exercise this afternoon at home carefully.*

Moreover, although we may begin the sentence with the time element, we may place neither the modifier of place nor of manner in initial position. Consequently we cannot say:

> *Carefully he wrote the exercise this afternoon at home.*
> *At home he wrote the exercise this afternoon carefully.*

It is not unreasonable to expect a further fixation and limitation of such patterns as time goes on.

Another kind of syntactical development concerns the shift in the function of inflection and auxiliary verbs. In the language of King Alfred, even in that of Chaucer, the auxiliary *can* literally and specifically meant 'to know' or 'to know how.' At that time the verb *may* was employed to indicate ability, where as the inflected subjunctive denoted possibility. At present, *can* indicates ability, *may* indicates possibility and upon occasion permission, and the inflected subjunctive has all but disappeared. In fact, *can* now often usurps the function of possibility and permission: *It could rain. Can I go?* Is the next step the disappearance of *may* and the replacement of *can* by some other construction?

Our present use of the verb *got* raises a series of similar questions. *Have got,* indicating possession, at times replaces *have,* which in turn displaced an earlier *owe, ought. Have got to,* meaning necessity or obligation is likewise taking the place of *ought* and *must.* Will these latter auxiliaries disappear altogether, as certain others, notably *thearf,* 'to need' and *dow,* 'to avail, befit' have done in the past? It is already evident that *going to* is encroaching upon the domain of *shall* and *will* to indicate future time.

Speculations of this nature might go on indefinitely, but at least some of the possible lines of development the English language may follow in the future have been suggested. To sum up: as possible developments in the English language of the next few centuries, we may expect that it will be spoken by more people, that it will include more words, that the pronunciations of its stressed vowels may change, that the noun plural and regular past tense inflections will be strengthened and that certain other inflections will gradually disappear, that there will be a continued fixation of word-order patterns, and a shift in some verb auxiliaries.

In considering the future of English one inevitably comes up against the question which has been one of the concerns of the present work, the differences between the language as spoken in England and in America. Will these become greater as time goes on, or will they tend to disappear?

This question can best be answered in terms of the particular facets of American culture which the preceding chapters have shown to be reflected in the English language as it is spoken here. We have seen that American English reflects, among other things, the melting pot aspect of American culture chiefly through

its verbal borrowings. By preserving some of the words, meanings, and features of the pronunciation of sixteenth- and seventeenth-century English, it mirrors the cultural lag so often reflected in a colony separated from the mother country by some
distance. The sinewy vigor of the frontiersman, his ingenuity
born of necessity, and his disregard of convention find their
counterpart in the bold creation of new compounds and derivatives, the free employment of functional changes, and the bizarre
blended forms; even his lusty humor is matched by his playfully hyperbolical tall talk. On the other hand, the glorification
of the commonplace and an accompanying tendency toward
euphemism betokens the squeamishness of a somewhat culturally
insecure middle-class and a mid-nineteenth-century deference to
feminine taste. To the extent that these culture traits are likely
to persist and be strengthened, it may be presumed that the language will continue to reflect them. When or as they become
less prominent their influence will diminish.

The verbal borrowings from immigrant nations have clearly
become less numerous. Many of our early loan words are now
obsolete, and the languages spoken by the bulk of our late nine-
teenth- and early twentieth-century immigrant peoples have left
little trace upon English. With immigration during the last three
decades reduced to a mere trickle, any further influx of borrowings beyond an occasional adoption here and there seems
unlikely. The retention of features of sixteenth- and seventeenth-
century English is not likely to be influenced greatly over the
years. There are few, if any, indications that our drugstore will
become a chemist's shop, or that the *r* coloring of our vowels will
grow less prominent. Though the gap between American and
British English in this respect is not likely to close, there are
certainly no indications that it will widen.

We shall undoubtedly continue to develop new compound
and derivative formations; word blending and functional change
will continue as active processes, but it must be remembered
that these are confined to certain quite definitely circumscribed
areas of the vocabulary. Many of our most ludicrous euphemisms

have already disappeared from current use, and on the question
of cultural insecurity we shall have something to say a little later.
All in all, there would seem to be little reason for anticipating a
further divergence between British and American English.

There is also the question of the extent to which British English is being influenced by Americanisms, a question which can
best be answered accurately and scientifically by one who speaks
British English. There is no question that the availability of
American books, newspapers, and films has served to acquaint
millions of Englishmen with American features of the language
which, however, they do not normally employ. Recognition or
passing acquaintance does not necessarily mean adoption, and
while it is possible here and there to point to English acceptance
and use of an American term, there is no more reason for expecting that American cooking and food terminology, political
jargon, or the lexicon of the automobile is going to be taken over
bodily than there is to suppose that the English are going to
cook like Americans or to alter their political organizations and
practices.

One must remember, however, that no matter how striking the
differences between British and American English may be, the
similarities far outweigh them, for it is in grammatical structure
and syntax—essentially the operational machinery of the language
—that the difference is negligible. It is neither exaggeration nor
idle chauvinism to say that the English language, with an exceptional past behind it, appears to be on the threshold of a still
greater future. Moreover, this future is to a considerable extent
in the hands of those who regularly speak and write the language. What can they do to insure and even to further the
development which lies ahead?

This basic question may best be answered by considering the
dangers which may conceivably beset a language in the particular
situation in which English finds itself today. There would seem
to be two such perils, diametrically opposed to each other. On the
one hand there are some who have seen, even in certain of the
developments which have been mentioned earlier in this chapter

—for example, the disappearance of the inflected subjunctive, the establishment of *who* in pre-verbal position, the use of *have got* to indicate possession—indications of a too great liberty, if not license. The unchecked development of tendencies such as these, it is argued, could lead to developments so divergent that the English language would lose its unity, and consequently its utility as a medium of communication. Opposed to this is the view that highly restrictive rules and conservative attitudes springing from a fear of solecism and leading to a denial of what is actual usage will exert such a confining influence upon the language that its flexibility will be lost and its ultimate potentialities remain unrealized.

Although there may be some danger from the first of these, the present social and cultural situation, in the United States especially, would seem to indicate that the greater of the two perils is the second. A number of factors enter into this situation. We have seen that from the beginning until late in the nineteenth century there was always a frontier, an area where unlettered pioneers toiled to secure cultural advantages for their children—including the mastery of Standard English. Moreover, the children of foreign-speaking immigrants felt the sting of social disapproval if their language betrayed their origin. The spread of higher education to social groups who in Europe would have remained comfortably within the confines of a regional or class dialect, also brought with it an emphasis upon correctness of speech and writing.

In learning a language, whether it be a different form of our native tongue or a totally foreign idiom, we operate inductively. We learn specific facts and usages first. When we have absorbed enough of these, we begin to synthesize—we form patterns, general behavior traits, upon which we then rely when a new situation faces us. The more uncertain we are of ourselves, culturally or in any other way, the more insistent we are upon guidance in specific facts and instances, and the more reluctant we are to rely upon an instinctive grasp of these general patterns. As far as raising the level of English is concerned, American textbooks

and teaching practices have too seldom taken the students
beyond the level of instruction in specific matters. As a consequence, most people in the United States carry about with them
a strange assortment of linguistic taboos. The feeling against
ain't, even as a first person interrogative, is very widespread.
Some react against *like* for *as*. For many the pronunciation *ice
cream* with primary stress on the first syllable is taboo; for others
the taboo against *John and me* so powerful that it prompts them
to use *John and I* even when it is structurally objective and *me*
would normally be demanded.

It may be reasonably argued that these taboos, which are after
all the results of a primarily negative approach to language, or
to expression, have performed their function and outlived their
usefulness. They should be replaced with something positive. We
are at a point where the doctrine of original sin, linguistically
speaking, must be replaced by a faith in intuition, by dependence
upon the established, unconsciously known patterns of the language. Such an instinct can be developed only by giving attention to the broader aspects of structure and the evolving tendencies of the language.

The history of English during the last two centuries demonstrates that highly restrictive and unrealistic rules of grammar
do not have a lasting effect upon the language as a whole. The
more incredible portions of the body of rules developed by
Nathaniel Ward, Dr. Johnson, Lindley Murray, and their followers have generally disappeared. In the present situation, however, the attitude behind the creation of a mass of non-pertinent
and unscientific linguistic legislation can still do positive harm.
It can create and preserve taboos, which ought never to have
been created, against certain expressions and constructions. It
can develop anxiety neuroses in many of the people who employ
the language. Both of these are undesirable conditions for the
future development of the English language. We cannot expect
a medium of communication to develop in advance of the cour-
age and resourcefulness of the people who employ it.

It is our responsibility to realize whither the language is tending, and the duty of our schools and teachers to promulgate healthy linguistic attitudes. If this is done, we may be certain that some individuals can and will attain greatness in the use of the language, which in turn will make of it a more flexible and sensitive medium for the rest of us. In this sense, a new era lies before all the English-speaking peoples.

APPENDIX

In order to indicate more specifically the sounds of spoken Elizabethan English than was feasible in the body of this work, Jaques' familiar speech on the Seven Ages of Man from *As You Like It* is given here in phonetic transcription. Many of the characters in the phonetic alphabet employed here have the same values which they normally have in our conventional spelling system ([o], [b], [z], etc.). Those characters which differ from the ordinary letters of the alphabet or which do not indicate the pronunciations usually associated with them are as follows:

VOWELS

  æ represents the sound of *a* in *mat.*
  æ: represents the sound of *a* in *sand* (as above, but of longer duration)
  e represents the sound of *a* in *fate.*
  ɛ represents the sound of *e* in *met.*
  i represents the sound of *ee* in *keep.*
  ɪ represents the sound of *i* in *bit.*
  ɔ represents the sound of *au* in *autumn.*
  ɔ: represents the sound of *a* in *call* (as above, but of longer duration)
  u represents the sound of *oo* in *food.*
  ʊ represents the sound of *oo* in *good.*
  ə represents the sound of *a* in *above, Cuba.*

CONSONANTS

g   represents the sound of *g* in *get*.
j   represents the sound of *y* in *yet*.
ŋ   represents the sound of *ng* in *sing*.
ʃ   represents the sound of *sh* in *shell*.
θ   represents the sound of *th* in *thin*.
ð   represents the sound of *th* in *then*.
tʃ represents the sound of *ch* in *choose*.
dʒ represents the sound of *g* in *gem*.
hw represents the sound of *wh* in *whale*.

THE SEVEN AGES OF MAN

ɔːl ðə wərldz ə stæːdʒ
ənd ɔːl ðə mɛn ənd wɪmən mɪrlɪ plæɪərz
ðæɪ əv ðər ɛgzɪts ənd ðər ɛntrənsɪz
ənd wʊn mæn ɪn ɪz təɪm plæɪz mɛnɪ pærts
ɪz ækts bɪɪŋ sɛvən æːdʒəz   ət fərst ðɪ ɪmfənt
mjulɪŋ ən pjukɪŋ ɪn ðə nərsəz ærmz
ðɛn ðə hwəmɪŋ skulbɔɪ wɪð ɪz sætʃəl
ənd ʃaɪnɪŋ mɔrnɪŋ fæːs krɪpɪŋ ləɪk snæɪl
ʊnwɪlɪŋlɪ tə skul   ən ðɛn ðə luvər
səɪŋ ləɪk fərnəs wɪð ə wofʊl bæləd
mæːd tu ɪz mɪstrɪs əɪbrəʊ   ðɛn ðə soldʒər
fʊl əv stræːndʒ oðz ən bɛrdəd lɔrk ðə pærd
dʒɛləs ɪn ɔnər   sʊdn ən kwɪk ɪn kwærəl
sikɪŋ ðə bʊbl rɛpjutæːsjən
ɪn ðə kænənz məʊθ   ən ðɛn ðə dʒʊstɪs
ɪn fæɪr rəʊnd bɛlɪ wɪð gʊd kæːpən ləɪnd
wɪč əɪz səvɪr ən bɛrd əv fɔrməl kʊt
fʊl əv wəɪz sɔːz ənd mɔdərn ɪnstənsɪz
ən so i plæɪz ɪz pært   ðə sɪksθ æːdʒ ʃɪfts
ɪntu ðə len ənd slɪpərd pæntəlun
wɪð spɛktəklz ɔn noz ən pəʊtʃ ɔn səɪd
hɪz juθfʊl hoz wɛl sæːvd ə wərld tu wəɪd
fər ɪz ʃruŋk ʃæŋk ənd ɪz bɪg mænlɪ vɔɪs
tərnɪŋ əgæm tɔrd tʃəɪldɪʃ trɛbl pəɪps

ənd hwɪslz ɪn ɪz səʊnd   læst sɪn əv ɔːl
ðət ɛndz ðɪs stræːndʒ ɪvɛntfʊl hɪstərɪ
ɪz sɛkənd tʃəɪldɪʃnəs ən mɪr əblɪvjən
sænz tiθ sænz əɪz sænz tæːst sænz ɛvrɪθɪŋ

INDEX

191